design ideas for
Flooring

CREATIVE HOMEOWNER®, Upper Saddle River, New Jersey

CRE▲TIVE
HOMEOWNER®

A Division of Federal Marketing Corp.
Upper Saddle River, NJ

DESIGN IDEAS FOR FLOORING

SENIOR EDITOR: Kathie Robitz
SENIOR DESIGNER: Glee Barre
ASSISTANT EDITOR: Evan Lambert
EDITORIAL ASSISTANT: Robyn Poplasky
FRONT COVER DESIGN: Glee Barre
PRODUCED BY: Home & Garden Editorial Services
AUTHOR: Joe Provey
LAYOUT: Jill Potvin Schoff
COPYEDITING: Jill Potvin Schoff, Owen Lockwood
EDITORIAL ASSISTANTS: Briana Porco, MaryAnn Kopp
PHOTO PREPRESS: Carl Weese
ILLUSTRATIONS: Bob La Pointe
INDEXER: MaryAnn Kopp
FRONT COVER PHOTOGRAPHY: *(top)* courtesy of Armstrong; *(bottom left)* courtesy of Ann Sacks Tile & Stone; *(bottom center)* courtesy of Armstrong; *(bottom right)* courtesy of Crossville Tile
INSIDE FRONT COVER PHOTOGRAPHY: *(top)* courtesy of Kemiko Concrete Products; *(bottom)* courtesy of Green Mountain Soapstone
BACK COVER PHOTOGRAPHY: *(top)* courtesy of Mannington Mills; *(bottom left)* courtesy of Teragren; *(bottom right)* courtesy of Expanko
INSIDE BACK COVER PHOTOGRAPHY: *(top)* courtesy of Armstrong; *(bottom)* Mark Samu

CREATIVE HOMEOWNER

PRESIDENT: Brian Toolan
VP/EDITORIAL DIRECTOR: Timothy O. Bakke
PRODUCTION MANAGER: Kimberly H. Vivas
ART DIRECTOR: David Geer
MANAGING EDITOR: Fran J. Donegan

Printed in China

Current Printing (last digit)
10 9 8 7 6 5 4 3 2

Design Ideas for Flooring, First Edition
Library of Congress Control Number: 2006924713
ISBN-10: 1-58011-309-5
ISBN-13: 978-1-58011-309-0

CREATIVE HOMEOWNER®
A Division of Federal Marketing Corp.
24 Park Way
Upper Saddle River, NJ 07458
www.creativehomeowner.com

Dedication

To MaryAnn, who helped make this book
possible in countless ways.

Acknowledgments

Special thanks to Jill Schoff for her invaluable contributions as
both copyeditor and layout artist, and to editorial assistant Briana Porco for handling myriad assignments with competence
and efficiency beyond her years. Thanks, too, to Bob La Pointe
for his beautiful illustrations, to Carl Weese for making the
book's photography look its best, and to the many flooring
manufacturers who contributed photos and expertise, especially
to Shaw Industries and Mannington Mills. Finally, thanks to
Floors Unlimited of Bridgeport, Connecticut, for suffering our
many questions and allowing us to photograph various types of
flooring in its showroom.

Contents

ABOVE Vinyl sheet in small mosaic is subtle and supremely functional.

RIGHT Linoleum, first popularized over 100 years ago, is now available with premade borders.

BELOW Bamboo, an ecologically sound alternative to wood, performs as well and often costs less.

Flooring has had its high and low points throughout history. About 2,000 years ago, Romans were popularizing tile as flooring throughout much of Europe. Egyptians were using stone millennia before that. In homes of the Middle Ages, however, floors were more likely to be hard-packed dirt and dung. Even 300 years ago, many American colonists walked on sand layered over dirt.

Flooring today, however, has entered a golden age. We can still use ancient materials, such as stone, tile, and mosaic, but we have hundreds of other choices as well. Some may surprise you: renewable "green"

Introduction

floors such as cork and bamboo, wood with exotic veneers, porcelain tile that needs no adhesive, laminates that come ever so close to nature, durable carpets made of leaf fiber and seagrass, and fiberglass-reinforced vinyl that you could pull up and hose down in the driveway if you had a mind to. Modern flooring is also much easier to install and maintain, thanks to higher manufacturing standards and incredibly durable finishes. We hope *Design Ideas for Flooring* will inspire you with examples of beautiful floors. And we hope our advice and resource listings will help you realize the perfect floors for your home.

Flooring is what you might call an intimate building product. You're almost always in contact with it. Consequently, you ask a lot from it. Flooring has to be comfortable and safe underfoot, spill- and moisture-resistant, easily cleaned, and durable. But that's not all: flooring is also a vital element of successful interior design. While rarely the focal point of a room, it is almost always in view. The right flooring choice can enhance your furnishings, cabinetry, and color scheme. The wrong choice can cheapen and detract from an otherwise beautifully decorated room.

Define Your Goals

❚ practically speaking ❚ design basics ❚
❚ taking measure ❚ safety and health ❚
❚ building a budget ❚

There are many choices when it comes to flooring, just as there are when designing the rest of your personal space. What to choose depends largely upon discovering what *you* want.

practically speaking

B egin the design process by asking a series of questions that will help you define your goals. Doing so will eliminate some choices and suggest others you haven't yet considered. For example, will the floor be subject to moisture, such as high humidity or spills and splashes? If so, a vinyl or tile floor is probably your best choice. If the moisture is not severe, laminate flooring or engineered-wood flooring may be okay as well.

How much traffic do you expect, and will it sometimes be wearing dirty shoes? Heavy traffic and dirt (because it's abrasive) require tough flooring, such as ceramic, stone, or vinyl tile. Less-trafficked areas are ideal for organics, such as wood, cork, laminate, and carpeting.

Other questions relate to health and comfort. Does anyone in your family suffer from allergies? Some flooring, such as cork, has natural antimicrobial properties. Hardwood floors are easy to keep dust free. You may want to avoid wall-to-wall carpeting. Are cold floors an issue? If so, you may want to rule out masonry products, such as tile—unless, of course, you opt for a radiant-floor-heating system as well. Is the floor in an area where you'd like to minimize noise? Carpeting and cork are quieter than wood or tile and good choices for rooms where kids play. Rubber flooring and other resilient floorings are also relatively quiet.

Convenience is a high priority with many busy homeowners. How important is low maintenance to you? In general, synthetic floors are easier to care for than natural floors—but not always. New finishes make it possible to put wood floors in nearly every room. And textured vinyl products, such as patterned tile with realistic grout lines, may be just as difficult to clean as natural flooring.

Once you've answered these questions, you will have narrowed your flooring options. Then the fun begins—because regardless of how many practical restrictions apply, you will still have countless flooring styles from which to choose.

TOP LEFT Top-quality laminate flooring, such as this plank style, is extremely durable and better suited to areas subject to moisture than real wood. No glue is required.

LEFT This engineered 3-in.-wide maple plank floor has a real maple veneer with a 25-year finish warranty. Only ⅜ in. thick overall, it installs with adhesive.

ABOVE The designer of this interior chose hard-wearing ceramic tile for the busy and messy kitchen zones, as well as the entry. Wood strips were used elsewhere.

BELOW Dirt can eventually grind its way through floor finishes. For dirt-prone areas, use a throw rug to catch abrasive particles. Shake out and vacuum the rug, clean it regularly.

ABOVE AND RIGHT Installing vinyl tiles and planks—such as this mudroom's realistic distressed oak—is relatively easy but requires a perfectly smooth substrate. Otherwise, bumps will "telegraph" to the finished surface.

BELOW Ceramic and stone tile are among the most difficult flooring materials to install. Rent a wet saw and blade to ease the job.

to diy or not

Successfully installing flooring yourself depends on two things: the product you choose and your skill level. Some materials, such as laminate and many vinyl products, require nothing more than careful measuring and the ability to cut a straight line with a utility knife or light-duty saw. Others demand more advanced skills, such as being able to use a circular saw to rip planks, a wet saw to cut ceramics, a power nailer to fasten solid wood flooring to a subfloor, or a notched trowel to apply just the correct amount of adhesive. The toughest floors require adding plywood, backer board, or a mortar bed prior to installation and solving flooring height problems that may arise at threshold and transitions. The latter should only be tackled by advanced do-it-yourselfers.

ABOVE Aside from laying down an area rug, the easiest floor to install is fiberglass-reinforced vinyl. It only needs to be cut to fit with a utility knife. In high traffic spots, manufacturers recommend securing it with double-faced tape.

LEFT To minimize noise, use carpeting, which is quieter than wood or tile and a good choice for rooms where kids play. Rubber, cork, and other resilient floorings are relatively quiet as well.

Aside from being functional, flooring must complement the decor of your room. If your style is Old World, hand-scraped wood flooring set off by substantial baseboard moldings may be the ticket. If your taste leans to contemporary, a simple design in solid vinyl tile or bamboo may appeal to you. Or, bring a country look to life with a quilt-inspired area rug.

Regardless of your preferred style, determine the dominant room element before making your selection. Perhaps it's the cabinetry in your kitchen, the poster bed you don't intend to let go or the sleek leather sofa for which you've just begun to make payments. The flooring you choose should complement, though not necessarily match, it. In fact, contrast is what often gives a room its visual appeal. In a kitchen, for example,

design basics

cabinets are often the dominant element. You may want to choose a contrasting flooring color or shade to help show off their beauty.

Choosing the right-scale flooring is also critical to a room's success. Most of us wouldn't stuff a small room with an oversized sofa and large armchairs. Similarly, stay away from using a large-scale flooring pattern in a small space. Conversely, don't cover an expansive living room or family room with a small, intricate pattern.

You can, however, tweak perceptions about room size with lines, patterns, and textures. Run linear patterns parallel with the longest dimension of a room, and it will appear longer. Run them perpendicular, and it will appear shorter. Change how a space is perceived with other patterns as well. Using a large checkerboard flooring in one section of a kitchen, for example, and a smaller checkerboard in a breakfast nook will make the nook look farther away. Strong textures and patterns can also "bring" flooring closer to the viewer, thereby making a room feel a bit more intimate. Solids, especially in light tones and neutral colors, can make flooring surfaces recede.

play checkers

Choose flooring that mirrors patterns in cabinetry, such as the way the vinyl floor in this kitchen reflects the wine cabinet.

LEFT The curtains, a dominant room element, provided the inspiration for this lively painted hallway floor.

RIGHT The wide planks on this bedroom floor are scaled to suit the bed's hefty posts and rails. They offer a nice contrast to the nightstand and bead-board panel in the footboard.

IIIII make flooring your common denominator IIIIIIIIIIIIIIII

floors as design anchors

Dark- and mid-toned floors are the easiest to make work in most room settings. That's because they provide a visual anchor or foundation that "frames" rooms and defines spaces. Dark floors can hold disparate elements together. White or very light-colored flooring, on the other hand, often makes dark furnishings and cabinets look as though they're floating. It can also be a source of glare in a brightly lit room. That said, a light-colored floor can be stunning in a room with lots of white, off-whites, and pale colors. The rule of thumb is: go with a light-colored floor if most of your furnishings and cabinetry are light, too. Feel free to disregard the rule if you're decorating a room that's small or has little natural light. In such spaces, light-colored floors can be used to make rooms feel bigger and more airy.

bright idea
go light

Use white, off-whites, and natural wood-look floors (this one is a laminate) to give small rooms a roomier feeling

ABOVE LEFT This dark-stained plank floor anchors a kitchen filled with mid- and light-toned elements. It also helps keep the kitchen from feeling too big.

OPPOSITE FAR LEFT In an open plan, a mid-tone floor is a good compromise. It integrates the dark appliances and countertop with the lighter cabinetry and nearby flooring.

LEFT Mid-tone planks ground this living room and dining room, while an area rug differentiates the spaces.

ABOVE Give a small space a roomier feel by using flooring—in this case, porcelain tile—to create diagonal lines. The diagonal lines lead the eye along a longer path than do lines in a grid. Using tile of varying sizes and orientation will also help to make a small room feel larger.

RIGHT In a long, narrow room, run flooring perpendicular to the long dimension to make the room look less like a corridor.

BELOW AND BOTTOM Floors can unify or divide. The large sisal rug joins the living and dining areas (below), while the contrasting tile and wood clearly show where the kitchen ends and the breakfast nook begins (bottom).

bright idea

set the stage

Use contrasts to create drama. The light floors and sofa in this family room are in perfect balance with the dark furniture, walls, and deep-colored area rug.

ABOVE Strong related colors, such as the copper of this vinyl sheet floor and the red accents, create a warm and secure feeling for many people.

LEFT If you plan to sell in the future, select materials and colors that are neutral and timeless so as to appeal to the largest percentage of potential buyers.

color & pattern

Bold geometric patterns have a vastly different effect than swirls and contours. They make the space feel more structured and organized. Variegated and speckled patterns create a softer feel than solids because they visually break up the surface plane. Monochromatic schemes, whether done in a light or deep tone, tend to be restful and calming. So are schemes created with analogous (closely related) colors, such as blue and green. Complementary color schemes (colors opposite one another on a color wheel) add movement and are often upbeat. Colors themselves affect people in different ways. Keep this in mind when selecting your flooring—but in the end go with what resonates with you.

▮▮▮ make color work ▮ ▮▮▮▮▮▮   ▮▮▮▮▮

ABOVE Complementary blues and oranges, such as in this room, make a strong statement and draw your attention.
▮

ABOVE RIGHT Warm reflected light from the floor will enhance skin tones, especially with the aqua walls as a backdrop.
▮

RIGHT Slate often displays many colors on its surface. Choose the one you want to emphasize, and find a paint to match for your walls.

Estimating the amount of flooring material you will need is not as simple as width times length, even when your room is rectangular or square. You must also consider the type of flooring, the standard sizes, pattern (if any), and how much waste (cutoffs you won't be able to use) you'll have. When in doubt, make an accurate diagram and bring it to the home center or flooring store for help with your estimate.

taking measure

For most floors, including wood, laminate, and tile of all types, multiply the length of the room by its width to get the area. If the room has an irregular footprint, such as an L-shape, divide the space into square or rectangular areas and then calculate the area of each section separately. Add the areas together to get the total area. Next, figure out how much square footage a carton of your flooring material will cover. (It's often given on the carton.) For example, 15 12 × 12-inch tiles per carton would come to 15 square feet. Divide the room's square footage by the carton's square footage to determine the number of cartons you'll need. Add about 10 percent for waste and the extra material you may need to make repairs in the future.

Estimating sheet flooring is a little different. If your room is less than 12 feet wide, look for a product that comes in 12-foot widths. You'll avoid the need for a seam, speed the installation, and save material. If your floor is wider than 12 feet, you will have to know the "repeat" measure for the pattern you've selected. The repeat is the length of extra material required to reach the start of the pattern. (See the drawing at the bottom of the opposite page.) If you don't account for the repeat, the pattern won't match up at the seam. If cabinets or a fireplace jut into the room, ignore them when figuring your square footage.

LEFT When planning the installation of a new floor, you will have to measure carefully, allow for waste, ensure proper preparation, and decide how to handle stairs, thresholds, transitions, and moldings.

estimating flooring needs

When measuring for tiles and boards, divide the floor into rectilinear sections (A, B, C, D) as shown in the illustration below; measure the area of each; and add them up to get floor area. With sheet flooring (bottom illustration), determine the roll width that will minimize seams. Then order enough lineal feet of sheet flooring to cover all of the areas wall to wall and to account for any extra you may need so that patterns align.

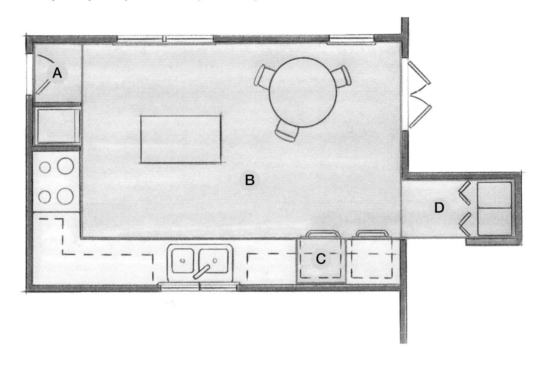

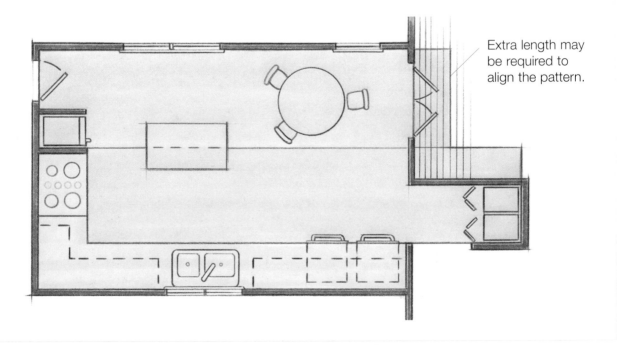

Extra length may be required to align the pattern.

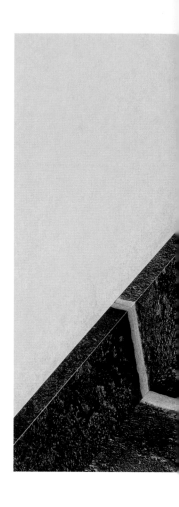

ABOVE Baseboard moldings hide the expansion gap that many flooring products require. The gap allows the flooring to expand and contract with changes in heat and humidity. When installing baseboard moldings, drive nails into the studs and plates as shown—not into the subfloor.

flooring preparation

When adding a new floor as part of a remodeling, you will need to evaluate several factors. If the old floor is smooth and solid and does not have a cushion backing as some vinyl sheet floors do, you may be able to leave it where it is and install your new floor on top. Minor bumps, voids, joints, and embossing may have to be made smooth by sanding or filling so that they do not "telegraph" or show through the new floor. (This is especially important when installing a resilient floor.)

When the substrate is very rough, manufacturers often recommend removal or covering it with ¼-inch plywood before proceeding with your installation. Of course, if adding plywood or a new layer of flooring will result in a significant height difference (more than ⅜ inch) between the new floor and adjacent floors, you may want to avoid creating a tripping hazard at thresholds and decide to remove the old floor to gain the depth your new floor requires. Caution: before removing any old, resilient floor (and the adhesive used to install it), test for asbestos. Releasing asbestos fibers into the home can be hazardous, so removal should be done by a licensed asbestos abatement company. Asbestos was used in many building products until it was banned in the late 1970s.

handling transitions

Decisions about transitions—changes from one surface to another—are best made before you begin your flooring project. Common transitions to consider include floor to floor, floor to stairs, floor to thresholds at interior and exterior doors, and floor to walls. Your decision will often depend on whether floor heights differ where they meet, whether the floor is subject to expansion, the kind of flooring material, and the style of the room. Here are several common transition solutions:

THRESHOLD

REDUCERS

FLOOR TRANSITION

CARPET TRANSITION

TOP Most flooring manufacturers offer a line of baseboard molding and transitions that coordiate with their products.

ABOVE There are many ways to redo flooring on steps, such as this overlap stairnose in laminate.

Flooring is not generally considered a home hazard, but there are safety and health issues of which you should be aware as you make your flooring product selections. The biggest hazard has to do with slips and falls in kitchens and bathrooms. In such areas, avoid glassy smooth surfaces, such as polished marble tiles set without grout joints. (Friction from the grout joints actually helps make a surface slip-resistant.) Tiles with matte finishes and textures offer more friction underfoot. Make area rugs more secure with a slip-resistant padding underneath. In the

safety and health

bathroom, use bathroom rugs with nonskid backing.

Mold will grow on virtually any type of flooring if it is dirty and the relative indoor humidity gets above 65 percent. In areas of the home where these conditions sometimes exist, it's wise to choose an easy-to-clean flooring surface (vinyl tile as opposed to carpeting, for example). The same goes for flooring in the homes of allergy sufferers. Choose a hard surface that's easy to clean, such as linoleum or wood. Area rugs, as long as they are light enough to shake or beat frequently, may also be used to help trap dust, dander, pollen, and mold spores. Avoid wall-to-wall carpeting, according to the American Institute of Family Physicians, unless you plan to be vigilant about keeping it well vacuumed.

OPPOSITE LEFT TOP Cork, aside from its being the ultimate comfort, offers excellent traction. Drop a glass, and it's likely to bounce, not shatter.

OPPOSITE LEFT BOTTOM Borders can serve as cautionary signals, such as at this bathroom's unexpected step between the lav and tub areas.

OPPOSITE Linoleum, made from natural ingredients, is a microbe fighter, is easy to clean, and outgases virtually no VOCs. (See "VOC," below.)

RIGHT Concrete floors, such as the one in this master suite, are ideally suited to radiant-floor-heating systems and to households where mold and allergens are concerns.

VOC

VOCs, or volatile organic compounds, are another health-related flooring concern. Small amounts will outgas (slowly be released) from many flooring products for months or years. VOCs include potentially harmful gases, such as formaldehyde. Outgassing can be minimized by using flooring (such as linoleum, solid wood, and ceramics), adhesives, and backings that do not outgas VOCs. Or, use vinyl products that have been certified as within acceptable limits by FloorScore, the Resilient Floor Covering Institute's (RFCI) voluntary product certification program.

ABOVE Highly textured vinyl, such as this mosaic sheet flooring, offers much more slip-resistance than smooth vinyl and ceramic tiles.

LEFT Carpeting on stairs and landings should be a tight weave and not heavily padded.

slippery subject

Flooring materials are measured for friction—and standards exist. The test is a bit Rube Goldbergish. With one testing machine, a shoe sole rests against an articulated arm that is attached to variable weights. When the weight is heavy enough, the shoe is pushed across the surface in question. A relative friction value is then assigned to the flooring. The truth of the matter is that other variables (primarily speed, wetness, and shoe sole material and texture) make the ratings less meaningful. For the record, however, The American Disabilities Act recommends a static coefficient of friction value of 0.6 for level residential flooring.

II put safety first IIIIIIIII

ABOVE Carpeting in a bath is a soft and slip-resistant alternative to a hard surface. Just don't invite the kids.

ABOVE RIGHT Don't rely on flooring to prevent tripping. Fully graspable stair rails are a must.

RIGHT If you must use marble in your bath, you're not alone. But opt for a honed finish, sizable grout lines, and inlaid listels (borders) to improve traction.

LEFT Tightly woven wall-to-wall carpeting offers the best slip resistance of any floor as long as it's properly stretched (no ripples or raised seams).

ABOVE Continous floors, such as these rubber tiles, at thresholds eliminate tripping hazards and make accessibility easier for people in wheelchairs.

LEFT BOTTOM Friction strips provide added safety for painted basement stair treads.

OPPOSITE Place nonslip matting under small rugs next to the bed to keep them from sliding or bunching and causing falls.

flooring for the elderly

If you live with someone who is elderly, consider additional precautions as recommended by the National Safety Council:

Avoid changes in flooring elevation wherever possible, and opt for smooth transitions between floor types to reduce the chance of accidental trips. You may want to remove thresholds as well. If that's not possible, signal height differences and level changes by varying colors and textures.

Avoid deep-pile and shag carpeting—it can cause falls when shoes, toenails, or walkers snag on them. A low-pile carpet is a good flooring choice throughout the house, even in the bathroom, where it can help cushion a dangerous fall.

Polished surfaces are a no-no. Not only are they slippery when wet, but the glare can be blinding. If you do choose a hard surface, keep in mind that small porcelain tiles in a matte finish and textured to be similar to stone are much less slippery than large, smooth tiles.

IIIIIIIIIIIIIIIIIIIIIIIII **safety is in the details** IIIIIIIIIIIIIII

bright idea

save the old

Strip and sand old molding for reuse with new flooring. Then repaint or stain it to save big bucks.

To figure out the cost of your project, you will need to know more than the flooring cost per square yard. Additional materials include carpet padding, building paper, underlayment, new molding, new thresholds, adhesives, grout, and finishes. Extra labor charges may include old floor removal and disposal or, if the old floor is being covered, repair work to make it smooth. If you're doing the job yourself, there will almost inevitably be some tools you'll need to buy or rent. To install tile, for example, figure on buying various types of trowels, tile nippers, a scoring tool, a chalk-line box, and safety gear (goggles, knee pads, and so on). You'll probably also want to rent a tile saw, which is available at most home centers.

building a budget

The table on page 34 gives price ranges for common flooring materials. Installed costs will be at least twice the cost of the material. A vinyl floor with a material cost of $15 per square yard may be more than $30 per square yard with installtion. Actual installed costs will vary greatly depending on the size of the job, the area in which you live, how much preparation your floor will require, and whether you do any of the work yourself. For a rough estimate of the complete job in your area, a helpful Web site is www.costestimator.com.

Don't confuse initial flooring costs with lifetime costs. For example, a low-grade vinyl sheet floor or low-grade carpet may be your cheapest option. If you're planning on staying in your home for many years, however, consider the overall costs. A ceramic floor will probably last the longest with the least amount of refinishing and care. Even if you don't plan to stay put, better-grade products will often allow you to recoup more of your investment upon resale. Wood flooring is a strong plus in many real-estate markets.

OPPOSITE TOP As the price of oil climbs, so does the cost of synthetic flooring, such as vinyl and synthetic carpeting. Flooring made from natural materials, such as wood and wool, become more cost competitive—and in some cases, less expensive.

OPPOSITE BOTTOM LEFT Stone floors are the most costly to have installed. Laminate flooring is among the least-expensive flooring, largely because preparation and installation are relatively easy.

ABOVE Flooring represents about 20 percent of the decorated area of a room (including ceilings) and at least that much of the typical room remodeling budget.

flooring costs

Type of flooring	Material costs per sq. yd.
Area rug (oriental, wool)	$80 to $800
Bamboo	$36 to $65
Ceramic tile	$18 to $70
Cork	$25 to $43
Decorative concrete	$2 to $150
Engineered wood	$27 to $80
Laminate	$13.50 to $35
Linoleum	$40 to $50
Hardwood (prefinished)	$27 to $50
Parquet (prefinished)	$23 to $58
Plastic tile	$27 to $45
Rubber tile	$18 to $45
Sheet vinyl	$4 to $16
Stone tile	$22 to $153
Vinyl tile (glue-down)	$9 to $25
Vinyl tile (self-stick)	$2.70 to $11
Wall-to-wall carpeting	$2.70 to $45

when hiring a pro

If you're planning to hire a flooring contractor, he will help you work up a budget. Just be sure to hire one that's reputable. Look for someone who has been in business for at least a few years and who has experience installing the flooring that you're buying. If the contractor won't do the work, find out who will (an employee or subcontractor, for example). Ask for references, and check that his workman's compensation and liability insurance are up to date. Ask for a contract that, in addition to total cost, specifies product, start and completion dates, and cleanup standards at the end of each work day, as well as how change orders will be handled. In addition, discuss how the job will be handled. Will the old flooring be removed? Moldings reused or replaced? How will thresholds and transitions be handled? Who is responsible for discarding old building materials? It's best to meet with several contractors before signing a contract with the one who, all things considered, you think will do the best job for a reasonable amount of money.

ABOVE LEFT AND OPPOSITE Whether you spend $250 on vinyl tiles (above left) and install them yourself or $2,500 for a pro to install porcelain tile (opposite), a new floor can enhance any room.

LEFT At less than $1 per sq. ft., self-stick vinyl tiles remain a low-cost solution.

| | | | | | | | | | | | plan for a successful installation | | | | | | | | | | | |

2

Nature is tough to top when it comes to growing beautiful materials. So it is with natural flooring. The textures and colors simply cannot be duplicated in synthetic material, even though today's sophisticated reproduction techniques come amazingly close. In addition to good looks, natural flooring products are very durable, made from renewable sources, are easy to repair or refinish, and can be recycled. On the flip side, natural flooring sometimes requires more maintenance. Don't worry, though—many manufacturers are producing prefinished products that are warranted for decades.

The Naturals

engineered and solid wood | **bamboo**
| **linoleum** | **cork** | **wool** |
| **other natural fibers** |

Wood flooring dominates the natural flooring category and is now available in more styles than in the past. This 5-in.-wide engineered plank has a cherry veneer stained to a deep amber color.

Wood flooring, always prized, has experienced a surge in popularity in recent years. Shipments in 2005 exceeded those of any year since 1966, according to NOFMA, the Wood Flooring Manufacturers Association. In addition to natural beauty, homeowners like it for its design versatility. Many feel that even if their furnishings change, the wood floors will complement the new decor. Wood is also a good insulator, making it warm underfoot. It is extremely durable and can be fairly easily repaired or refinished.

Wood flooring is available in two types, solid and engineered. Solid wood is just that; it's joined with a traditional tongue and groove. Properly maintained, it will last indefinitely. Engineered wood products combine several layers of real wood. They are less thick, more stable, and easier to install. Their topside veneers come in dozens of species, including exotic woods rarely used for flooring in the past.

engineered and solid wood

Solid-wood flooring is not recommended for moisture-prone areas, such as basements and baths—or in climates with high humidity. Engineered wood is less susceptible to moisture and may be installed in a greater range of locations, including below grade. Check the manufacturer's recommendations beforehand. Some engineered flooring has locking tongues and grooves and can be floated over an existing floor. Others must be glued in place.

Solid-wood flooring is available in strips, planks, or parquet, finished or unfinished. Strip thicknesses range from 5/16 to 3/4 inch, widths from 1½ to 2¼ inch. Planks are ½ to 3/4 inch thick and 3 to 8 inches wide. Strips and planks may be milled from various parts of the tree. Quartersawn boards, for example, are cut from logs that have been quartered. They are generally more stable and the grain patterns more subtle—especially the boards cut from the tree's heartwood, or core. Parquet, typically a square panel, is composed of small wood slats joined by adhesive and fasteners.

Engineered wood generally comes in 3- to 6⅛-inch-wide prefinished planks of single or random lengths. Overall thickness ranges from ¼ to 3/4 inch, depending upon the manufacturer. Plies range from two to ten. The more plies, the more stable the product. But the key issue when buying engineered wood products is the thickness of the veneer layer. If it's too thin, it can't be refinished. Look for a product with at least a ⅛-inch veneer. You'll be able to refinish it one or two times.

LEFT The celebration of solid-wood flooring in this great room enhances both the owners' enjoyment and the value of their home.

BELOW LEFT Engineered wood flooring is the smart choice in damp locations and humid climates.

BELOW Wood floors date to the Middle Ages, when rough planks were scraped smooth with metal blades or rubbed with stones. Today the hand-scraped look is back in vogue and available in both solid and engineered wood products (shown).

RIGHT More prefinished flooring, such as the wide planks with beveled edges shown here, is installed today than unfinished floors. Top-of-the-line engineered wood products have a birch ply core.

OPPOSITE TOP Prefinished floorboard edges are available with varying degrees of chamfering (commonly called beveling) and rounding-over (or easing). Beveled edges (shown) help to disguise slight variances in floorboard height. With site-finished floors, this is not an issue because the entire surface is sanded flat.

OPPOSITE BOTTOM Engineered wood is basically plywood (or dense fiberboard) with a veneer on top.

wood floor types

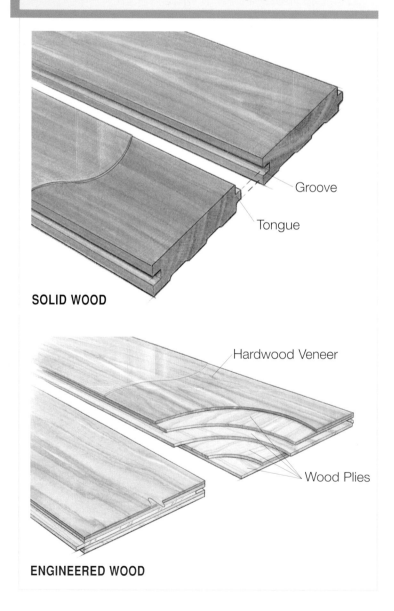

Groove

Tongue

SOLID WOOD

Hardwood Veneer

Wood Plies

ENGINEERED WOOD

bright idea

prefinished

Choose prefinished wood flooring. It installs faster than site-finished flooring—and you won't have to stay off it for a week or more while the finish dries. Nor will it produce odors during the curing time.

wood floor grades

NOFMA,* The Wood Flooring Manufacturers Association, certifies that wood flooring produced by its members adhere to strict quality control in regard to length, width, thickness, squareness, tongue-and-groove location, and moisture content. In addition, its members use the same grading standards: Clear, Select, No. 1 Common, and No. 2 Common. Any grade will provide a serviceable floor, but the better grades, such as Clear and Select, will have fewer knots, color variations, mineral streaks, and manufacturing marks. Clear-grade flooring is milled from the heartwood (center) of trees, while the other grades are a mix of heartwood and sapwood.

*NOFMA actually stands for National Oak Flooring Manufacturers Association.

tough finishes

Today's most durable finishes are applied at the factory. Minute crystals of aluminum oxide or some other hard, clear mineral are embedded in layers of UV-cured urethane coatings. Such finishes are generally far more durable than site-applied finishes—although site-applied aluminum oxide finishes are now becoming available. Finish warranties go up to 25 years for both solid and engineered wood flooring products.

Despite improved finishes, proper care for wood floors is important. Keep your floors vacuumed (with the soft brush attachment) or swept to remove dirt, and follow the manufacturer's recommendation with regard to cleaners. Avoid wetting wood flooring, and in the event of a spill, don't allow the floor to stay wet for long. Avoid using oil soaps, vinegar, or disposable floor wipes. Flooring professionals can recommend safe wood-floor cleaners and mops.

OPPOSITE New finishes for wood floors are available in dozens of appetizing colors, including toffee, truffle, and cinnamon oak (shown here).

ABOVE In a Colonial setting such as this, a No. 2 Common grade flooring with large knots is appropriate and even desirable.

LEFT Today's new aluminum oxide wood finishes, available on both solid and engineered products, will hold up even to the abuse of a home office, with its constant shuffling of chairs and traffic.

RIGHT High contrasts in grain pattern, such as in the hickory shown, can be used to enhance a rustic decor.

bright idea

reclaim

Work with flooring manufacturers or local recyclers who reclaim wood that has been salvaged from condemned buildings, old logging sites, or even river bottoms. Old-growth wood is often of a quality that is no longer available. Old fasteners are removed, and the recovered materials are milled for use as flooring.

OPPOSITE TOP Wood flooring, especially as engineered products, is available in more species than ever before, including merbau (left) and cherry (right).

OPPOSITE BOTTOM This engineered plank has beveled edges and an antiqued and weathered hickory veneer. Floated over a subfloor, this product does not require glue.

wood hardness ratings

Wood is rated by relative hardness, with the harder species being the more durable, but actual hardness may vary depending on when and where the wood was grown.

Douglas Fir, 660	Australian Cypress, 1375	Grapia, 2053
So. Yellow Pine (loblolly & short leaf), 690	Bamboo (natural), 1380	Burma Mahogany, 2170
So. Yellow Pine (longleaf), 870	Hard Maple, 1450	Amberwood, 2200
Black Cherry, 950	Wenge, 1630	Santo Mahogany, 2200
Teak, 1000	Brazilian Oak, 1650	Mesquite, 2345
Black Walnut, 1010	Peruvian Maple, 1700	Brazilian Cherry, 2350
Bamboo (carbonized), 1180	African Pedauk, 1725	Peruvian Cherry, 2350
Heart Pine, 1225	Hickory/Pecan, 1820	Red Walnut, 2450
Yellow Birch, 1260	Kempas, 1854	Brazilian Teak, 3540
Red Oak (Northern), 1290	Purpleheart, 1860	Lapacho, 3670
American Beech, 1300	Jarrah, 1910	Patagonian Rosewood, 3840
Ash, 1320	Merbau, 1925	Brazilian Tiger Mahogany, 3840
White Oak, 1360	African Rosewood, 1980	Curupy, 3880

Bamboo, introduced as flooring in the early '90s, has captured a significant share of the market with its clean Asian look. A grass, it has the obvious advantage of quick, renewable growth—up to four feet in a day! Produced mostly in Asia, it is about as hard as oak and somewhat less expensive. Bamboo products have fewer markings than hardwood, for a clear look, although some products have lots of joint markings. In addition, bamboo is generally available in longer lengths (6 feet) than solid-hardwood flooring, for an unbroken appearance.

bamboo

Bamboo flooring is built up from thin strips or fiber. The strips can be vertically or horizontally arranged. Recently introduced strand-woven bamboo is made by reconstituting bamboo fiber as boards. Vertical styles, which don't show pronounced joint markings, are the most popular. Horizontal styles are sometimes engineered, with a bamboo veneer bonded to wood plies. Some products are prefinished top and bottom or on all six sides for better resistance to moisture. Installation is similar to installed solid and engineered wood products. Engineered bamboo flooring can be floated over an underlay pad for a cushioned step.

Because bamboo is a relatively new flooring product with no agreed upon grading system as of yet, it's wise to buy only from a reputable manufacturer. Product quality varies greatly. For example, quality bamboo flooring is harder than oak. An inferior product, often because the bamboo was harvested too early, can be as soft as pine. Adhesives used to bond the bamboo strips into planks can vary, too. Some emit high levels of volatile organic compounds (VOCs); others comply with or exceed the most stringent standards for indoor air quality. Ask for the latter.

OPPOSITE Bamboo is at home in contemporary and minimalistic settings, such as this kitchen area.

RIGHT Typically available in ⅝-in.-thick planks, widths vary from 3⅝ to 7½ in.

BOTTOM RIGHT Strand-woven products look very much like hardwood but with finer grain patterns and fewer knots.

BELOW Bamboo is available in dozens of stained colors. More commonly it comes in natural or carbonized (also called carmelized) finishes, in which the bamboo has been heated to create deeper tones.

types of bamboo

Bamboo flooring is available in several styles. Horizontally laid strips show characteristic joint markings and have fewer seams. Vertically laid strips have fewer markings but more seams. Engineered bamboo flooring usually has a veneer layer of horizontally laid bamboo. Strand-woven bamboo shows no seams and looks more like hardwood.

HORIZONTAL BAMBOO

VERTICAL BAMBOO

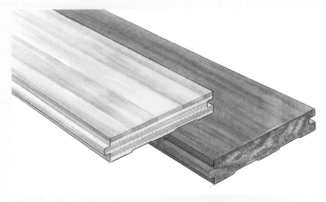

ENGINEERED AND STRAND-WOVEN BAMBOO

BELOW Square-edged planks, as used in this entry hallway, will prevent moisture infiltration better than those with beveled edges. To maintain bamboo, vacuum it regularly and go over it with a damp mop as necessary.

OPPOSITE TOP LEFT Engineered bamboo flooring is suitable for use with radiant heating.

OPPOSITE TOP RIGHT Good-quality bamboo matches up to oak in hardness and is more dimensionally stable. It can even be glued directly to a concrete subfloor.

OPPOSITE BOTTOM Horizontal bamboo flooring, such as in this dining room, shows the characteristic joint markings of bamboo.

Cork flooring, first developed in the late 1800s, is made from bark harvested from cork trees in Europe and northern Africa. Cork is renewable because the trees do not die and the bark can be harvested again after about 15 years. The cork material, shorn of its rough exterior layer, is ground up and mixed with binders before being formed into large blocks and baked. The blocks are sliced into tiles or veneers.

Cork, a favorite of notable architect Frank Lloyd Wright, has many properties that make it an excellent flooring material. Its resiliency makes it easy on the feet and resistant to damage by impact. In addition, cork flooring reduces noise and vibration, resists mold and mildew, is insect resistant, and offers good traction. It is normally finished with a matte-finish polyurethane (the wisest and most durable choice), acrylic, or wax.

cork

Cork flooring is available in dozens of inviting colors and textures, making it ideal for designing custom floors. Traditional 12 × 12-inch cork tiles are typically ³⁄₁₆ to ⁵⁄₁₆ inch thick and available prefinished or unfinished. They must be secured to either smooth primed concrete, plywood, or smooth existing flooring, either with troweled-on or contact adhesive. Newer, engineered cork planks (12 × 36 inches) can be floated over any surface with the manufacturer's recommended underlayment and vapor barrier. As with other engineered products, a veneer is glued to a high-density fiberboard core.

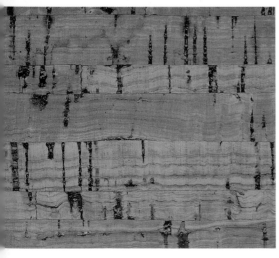

OPPOSITE LEFT Cork tiles are available in a wide variety of styles, from light and dark chunks (top) to natural (bottom).

OPPOSITE Use cork sheets to create custom patterns, such as diagonal stripes.

BELOW Cork can be made to have a granite texture (top) or mixed with rubber to become even more resilient and add colors (bottom).

RIGHT Cork complements the Old World charm of this library room.

bright idea
punch
Alternate dark, solid, and striated cork tiles to add punch to a floor.

RIGHT Diamond insets and a wide border help update this Victorian dining room.

BELOW Cork is especially effective with Arts and Crafts decor and timber-frame construction.

linoleum

Linoleum, a common flooring in the United States from 1900 to 1950, has made a bit of a comeback in the past two decades. Designers love it for its vibrant colors and retro feel, but its high cost has limited its popularity. Made from linseed oil, resins, cork powder, wood flour, ground limestone, pigments, and a jute backing, linoleum is environmentally friendly and wears well. It will even stand up to office chairs on casters. Linoleum is colorfast, and the colors and patterns go completely through the wear layer. As a bonus, it naturally inhibits the growth of some microorganisms, repels dust and dirt, and is antistatic.

Linoleum is generally not recommended for below-grade installations but can be used just about anywhere else, including kitchens and bathrooms. Available in tile and sheet products, styles range from solid colors to many marble and stone-like textures. The colors are intense and sumptuous. Maintenance is with a vacuum and a damp mop. Harsh alkali cleaners, as well as products with ammonia, should be avoided.

plank linoleum clicks

Easy-to-install plank linoleum is a tongue-and-groove flooring that floats on the subfloor or old existing floor. No adhesives are required. The tiles and planks are available in 12 x 12-inch and 12 x 36-inch shapes and can be arranged in a multitude of patterns, such as the design at right. A cork backing improves resiliency and reduces sound transmission.

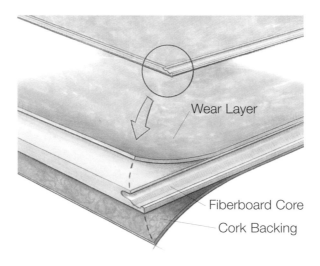

Wear Layer

Fiberboard Core

Cork Backing

ABOVE LEFT
Random use of tiles
in complementary
colors creates a
stunning family
room floor.

ABOVE This attic
retreat's floor was
created mostly with
planks; tiles form
the intersections.

RIGHT Linoleum is
an ideal product for
creating custom
kitchen floors.

ABOVE Choose from a vast palette of intense and pastel colors when planning your linoleum floor.

BELOW This minimalistic living room gets its pizzazz from a pastel linoleum rainbow.

bright idea
ready-made
Add ready-made borders to customize a linoleum floor. They are available in many patterns but should be installed by a professional.

choose linoleum for beautiful colors

BELOW Bold blue and off-white stripes are perfect for a beachside kitchen.

In 1000 AD, Marco Polo discovered rug making in central Asia. Fortunately, you don't have to go so far. Home centers with carpeting departments and retailers abound. So does a dizzying variety of types and styles. To help simplify things, you can read about and see examples of natural fiber carpets and rugs, such as wool and sisal, here. Synthetic-fiber products are covered in the next chapter.

wool

Wool, the ultimate animal fiber, is very soft, resilient (bouncing back even after furniture has been placed on it), easy to clean, a good insulator for both heat and sound, and extremely long lasting. Wool repels water but will absorb water vapor, helping to make it resistant to static electricity and fire. Carpets woven from wool have a soft, luxurious feel and come in a wide variety of colors and textures, from plushy cut-pile Orientals to high-loop and multi-level looped berbers. At home with traditional, contemporary, or casual styles, wool carpeting is often competitive with synthetic carpeting. And unlike hard-surface flooring, it requires little preparation (other than padding) before installation. One more difference: when you buy carpeting as an area rug, you can take it with you when you move.

OPPOSITE Area rugs made with wool from New Zealand come in styles to suit every decor, from traditional to contemporary.

LEFT Area rugs—wool and otherwise—have experienced greater sales as the popularity of wood flooring has grown.

broadloom **w**ool

The majority of wool carpets are sold as area rugs, although wool is making a comeback in the form of wall-to-wall carpeting.

Wilton carpets, such as these, are usually woven on a Jacquard loom and can include up to five colors in their designs.

This subtle trellis design, available in the latest colors, is a stylish compromise between classic and trendy.

ABOVE Broadloom carpeting can be sized and cut to your specifications for use as a large area rug, as shown. The edges can be bound with narrow or wide binding tapes in cotton, linen, and other materials. With wide bindings, opt for padding, hidden stitching, and mitered corners. Wide rugs may require a seam.

This colorful floral, in an Axminster weave, lends itself to contemporary or traditional decor.

bright idea
layered look

Lay small area rugs on larger carpets for an Old World look and a luxurious feel underfoot.

A heavy-gauge pile, such as this, is great for high-traffic areas. This one is blended with metallic yarn to make a carpet that stands out from the pack.

LEFT Area rugs in natural fibers, such as this flat-weave cotton, have gained in popularity along with wood floors—partly in a role as a floor protector.

BELOW LEFT This wool rug is part of a collection of reversibles and is available in sizes up to 12 ft. wide.

BELOW Casual sisal carpets make you feel as though you live near the ocean, even if you're miles away.

LEFT Cut linen pile and tone-on-tone coloring give these carpets an organic look.

BELOW Silk and wool combine for a radiant effect in this twist on Tibetan rugs.

other natural fibers

Natural-fiber carpets are also being made from a wide variety of plants and even from paper. Cotton rugs are quite common. They can provide a bright, cheerful accent, but don't expect them to withstand more than a few years of traffic. Linen-fiber carpets are much more durable and often have a natural, organic look.

Silk and silk combined with wool make wonderful (though expensive) carpets best suited to low-traffic and personal spaces. Sisal yarns are spun from long rope-like fibers of agave leaves, usually grown on plantations in East Africa and Brazil. They are smooth and durable, can be dyed to a wide variety of colors, and are naturally resistant to static electricity and fire. Sisal carpets often have a latex backing and come in a variety of textures and patterns. They are best suited for casual or earthy decors. Seagrass carpets are made from various grass-like plants that grow in marshy fields of South Asia. They are typically undyed, ranging in color from sage to greenish tan. They offer an inexpensive neutral accent to natural settings. Keep in mind that seagrass is susceptible to moisture and should be used only in dry areas. Jute, made from the bark of jute plants, is lustrous, tough, and soft. Jute yarns can be fine or rope-like and make for strong textural elements for informal settings. Paper carpets, woven from tightly twisted lengths of paper, produce smooth coverings with a calm, quiet feel. They are available in natural as well as colored products and are surprisingly durable.

RIGHT AND BELOW A large sisal carpet, backed with latex, is an economical way to cover expansive spaces, such as this living room-dining room combination. Sisal carpet edges are usually bound with linen, although there are many other choices, including leather.

OPPOSITE TOP LEFT Seagrass carpets are made from the fiber of any number of plants that grow in the marshes of South Asia.

OPPOSITE TOP RIGHT Sisal is the best-known natural plant fiber aside from cotton and linen. That its look is frequently copied in synthetic fiber is testimony to its popularity.

OPPOSITE This beautiful weave combines seagrass and corn husk.

3

The flooring materials of antiquity—tile and stone—are still with us. Whether used in a classic, rustic, or contemporary decor, they provide a reassuring sense of permanence. And that sense is real. Properly installed, these materials can last a lifetime, so double and triple think your choice. It's not going anywhere unless you tire of it. Modern production methods and sealers have made these materials easier to install and care for than in the past—and have helped reduce their installed cost. Still too expensive? You can get amazing tile-like or stone-like results with concrete floors.

Stone & Tile

| stone |

| decorative concrete |

| ceramic and porcelain tile |

The stone look is in—but look closely and you're likely to find it's porcelain, as in this kitchen. Porcelain tiles are easier to install and care for than stone, and a lot less expensive, too.

stone

Stone is without a doubt beautiful and enduring, but not long ago its use as flooring was pretty much limited to slate in the foyer and marble thresholds in bathrooms. In recent years, however, it has become popular in other home locations, especially in bathrooms. Stone tiles, primarily made from limestone, marble, granite, and slate, are available in a surprising number of colors, from off-whites and creams to blues, reds, greens, and golds. In addition, you can choose from over two dozen finishes, including cleft, tumble, sandblasted, etched, and flamed. See "Stone Finishes," page 73.

Travertine tiles also have gained in popularity and become more affordable. Travertine is a smooth but porous stone (the tiny holes can be filled or left open for a natural look) that's formed from mineral-laden water of underground rivers and springs and other types of subterranean moisture. Used since antiquity (including to build Rome's Colosseum), it has a timeless beauty and is readily available in several finishes, from tumbled to polished.

Terrazzo is yet another option, although it is primarily found in commercial applications, such as airports. It is an agglomerate made from waste produced by quarrying stone and is bound with cements or epoxies. Terrazzo tiles are about the same cost as better-quality ceramic tiles.

Stone floors require more maintenance than ceramic tile, including regular cleaning, occasional intensive cleaning, and sealing or impregnating with silicone. Sealers and silicone impregnators help prevent water or spills from penetrating and staining the stone. Finally, stone is typically more expensive than ceramic and porcelain tiles that look very similar.

OPPOSITE FAR LEFT This is just one of the dozens of granite colors available.

LEFT Slate, once limited to foyer floors and patios, is now front and center. It's shown here in a dramatic "roof shingle" style kitchen floor.

ABOVE Most travertine tile is cream colored, such as in this bathroom, but the available spectrum runs from white to deep mahogany.

plan ahead for stone

Although worth the effort, stone floors often require more planning and preparation than other types of floors. They are more difficult to install due to weight, greater thickness than tile, and variations in thickness within the same lot of stone. A mortar bed, often deeper than the one used for tile, is often required. This in turn may create problems when transitioning to other rooms with lower floor heights—unless you're building a new house, of course, and can plan all of your floor heights ahead of time.

know your stone

ABOVE Stone comes with many intriguing patterns, including this watery marble.

RIGHT Slate, too, comes in many colors. Lay out your tiles carefully to ensure a pleasing distribution.

bright idea

fixed in stone

Use marble and limestone in a tumble finish to create a permanent "bath mat."

popular stone styles

Tap into nature's array of texture and colors with stone, such as **granite**.

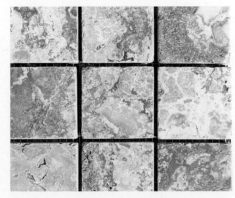

Textures run from chunky to smooth, as with this **finely textured granite**.

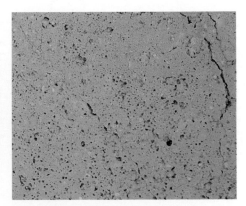

Travertine has open pores. It's also available with the pores filled.

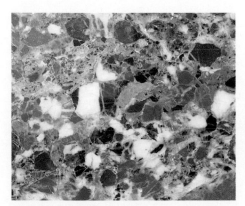

Tumbled limestone has a soft matte appearance and is slip-resistant.

This sample shows a **variegated form of travertine** in a tumbled finish.

Marble comes in an infinite number of swirling, or veining, patterns.

RIGHT The mixed quartz stones used for this bathroom's floor and walls were quarried and then tumbled smooth before being assembled into mesh-backed sheets. Similar tiles are available with other types of stone, including marble, basalt, and onyx.

go to the source

Purchasing stone can be something of an adventure. The quality of stone can vary from one source to another, and there are no industry standards. The best advice is to visit your local stone supplier and see the lot you're buying. There is too much variation from one lot to another to trust a sample or two. There are also a multitude of finishes that must be seen and felt to be understood. In general, they fall into two camps: degrees of smoothness and methods of distressing. (See the next page for a partial listing of finishes.)

stone finishes

Brushed: produced by a coarse, rotary wire brush.

Bushhammered: roughened with a bushhammer for decoration or to provide traction.

Flamed: a smooth but pebbled finish produced with a flame.

Grit-blasted or grit: a smooth nonreflective finish done mostly on marble and limestone.

Groove textured: small narrowly spaced grooves running across the stone surface. Also called a tooled finish.

Honed: a smooth hand- or machine-rubbed finish on stone, just short of polished.

Nicked bit: produced by planing with a tool that has irregular nicks in the cutting edge.

Plucked: obtained by rough planing the surface of stone, breaking or plucking out small particles to create a rough texture.

Polished: a smooth glossy finish—available on hard, dense stones only—that brings out the color and character of the stone.

Riven: a rough surface created when stone is split along natural cleavage planes.

Rubbed: between a smooth machine finish and a honed finish. Produced by mechanical rubbing.

Sandblasted: available in degrees of texture, from coarse to fine. Produced by blasting with an abrasive material.

Sawn: any of a variety of finishes produced by the sawing process. Similar to sawn textures on wood.

Semirubbed: a rough and smooth finish achieved by rubbing high spots off the surface.

Tumbled: obtained by rotating precut pieces of marble or limestone in a mixer or other container to round edges and smooth surfaces.

POLISHED

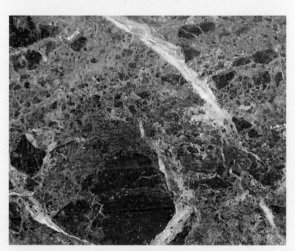

HONED

BRUSHED

decorative concrete

Concrete floors don't have to be gray. New materials and techniques can transform them into works of art. Acid staining, for example, can create beautiful marble- and stone-like patterns. The stain reacts chemically and permanently bonds with the minerals in the concrete to create an instant aged look. For more elaborate designs, grooves are sawn in the concrete to create patterns or decorative accents. The finished floor can be coated with wax, which will need renewing every couple of years in high-traffic areas, and buffed. Or it can be sealed for a higher sheen. Sealed concrete, however, is more likely to show scratches than waxed concrete.

For rough or out-of-level concrete floors, or for floors that have adhesive or markings that cannot be completely removed, thin coats of polymer-modified Portland cement will make them look better than new. These products are ideal for the garage and basement but can be used over old flooring, including vinyl asbestos tiling. With applied thicknesses ranging from 1 or 2 inches to feather-thin, these products are often self-leveling (no troweling) and quick drying. In addition, overlayments can be colored, textured, and scribed to simulate brick, tile, slate—or wherever your imagination takes you. When coupled with radiant heat in the floor, cold floor temperature is no longer an issue.

OPPOSITE To create the look of marble with this concrete floor, narrow "grout" lines were cut with a circular saw and masonry blade.

ABOVE Curved lines are more difficult to cut and must be planned out carefully. A different acid stain was used between each line.

LEFT This acid-stained medallion is centered around the support column of this basement recreation room.

diy **c**oncrete **f**loor

It is possible to acid-stain concrete yourself, if you're good at reading directions carefully. The process includes cleaning the surface thoroughly, taping off areas that you don't want stained, applying the stain in a cloud-like pattern (two coats), cleaning the resultant residue from the chemical reaction, and then waxing or scaling. Cost for the materials is less than $3 per square yard.

OPPOSITE Decorative concrete floors are popular in areas where houses or condominiums are built on concrete slabs. Grooving and acid staining in three colors create an elegant look for this traditional dining room.

TOP LEFT Few flooring types can equal the rich color of acid-stained floors—especially at decorative concrete's low cost per square foot.

LEFT Acid stains create earthy, muted tones. For brighter colors, other nonacid stains are available, though they do not bond chemically with the concrete and must be protected with a finish to prevent wear.

BELOW LEFT AND RIGHT Here are two examples of a polymer-modified cement overlay. Each was poured over existing flooring in ⅛-in. layers. Decorative work was done to the cured surface, and a protective acrylic finish was then applied.

Man-made tile is extremely durable, resistant to moisture, nonflammable, easier to install and less costly than stone. It's available in hundreds of shapes and styles, including stone patterns that are extremely realistic. On the other hand, tile is often cool and hard to the touch. Drop something fragile on it, and it will likely break. Drop something heavy, and the tile may crack. While tiles clean easily, the grout lines between them do not.

There are two main types of manufactured or handmade tile: ceramic and porcelain. Ceramic tile is made from various clays that, when fired, create a hard but porous surface. Porcelain is made from finer particles and fired at higher temperatures for longer periods than ceramic tile. The final result is a harder, denser product. Both types have their advantages. Ceramic tile is a little easier to cut for installation. When protected with a high-grade glaze, it will resist wear and scratches. Porcelain is harder and may have the same coloration (through-body color) through the tile—an advantage if it chips.

Ceramic and porcelain tiles are available in glazed or unglazed finishes. The glaze, a concoction of various minerals, is applied to the tiles before being fired in a kiln. It is what makes ceramic tile impervious to water. It also imparts color, texture, and design pattern, if any. Porcelain tiles, even unglazed, resist water. Manufacturers may glaze them anyway to create color, pattern, and texture. Glazes can be opaque or transparent, letting the color of the source clay come through. They may also vary in degree of gloss, from high gloss to matte. Unglazed ceramic tiles have no protective finish and will need to be sealed regularly.

ceramic and porcelain tile

RIGHT Many tiles today, such as these two porcelain tiles, are made to resemble stone.

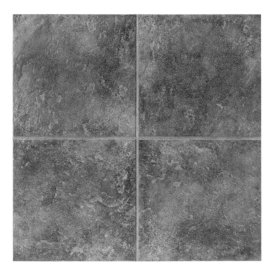

ABOVE Use porcelain tiles to construct a bold "carpet," complete with borders. Chiseled tile edges and a matte finish give it a vintage European look.

ABOVE RIGHT Popular ceramic and porcelain tile looks include marble, granite, and limestone—the latter is shown here.

RIGHT This family room's ceramic floor has the look of black granite set off by a stone mosaic border.

LEFT Ceramic tiles in beige and brown give this bathroom a warm, restful feeling. The use of two different-size tiles, two orientations, and a border adds texture to the room.

tile to suit every style

For a quiet, calm look, try porcelain tiles in a **stylized wood look**.

Vibrant **translucent glass mosaics** are just one of many glass tile styles.

Metal-covered porcelain tiles are effective as accents.

Porcelain tiles are sometimes "punched" prior to firing to impart a cleft texture.

A combination of glazes gives this **porcelain tile** a quarried look.

Ceramic tiles in earth tones and muted colors are popular.

tile ratings

Ceramic, stone, and porcelain tiles are rated in several ways. The Mohs Hardness Test, used since 1822, classifies a surface's ability to withstand scratching by minerals with differing degrees of hardness. Ten is the highest rating and has the hardness of a diamond. For residential purposes, a rating of 5 is usually sufficient to ensure good wear resistance. The Porcelain Enamel Institute (PEI) scale, a more precise test, rates surfaces from I to V, with V being hard enough for commercial, high-traffic situations. A PEI rating of III will handle medium residential traffic, including entryways, kitchens, and stairs. Ask about a tile's installed break strength as well; it is measured in pounds per square inch.

| | | | | | choose from tiles that look like stone and more | | | | | | |

ABOVE Handmade terra-cotta tiles (shown) and Mexican tiles need to be sealed to prevent staining—but they can't be rivaled for an authentic, rustic look and feel.

LEFT Solid-wood planks and handmade tiles make a stunning combination.

ways to install tile

Porcelain and ceramic tile can be installed over concrete slabs or over a wood subfloor if it is solid (little or no deflection). Otherwise, movement in the floor could cause cracks. When installing tile over a wood subfloor, the preferred method is to lay down a bed of reinforced mortar first. The tile is then bonded to the mortar with adhesive. As this can raise a floor height by more than 1 inch to over 2 inches and is quite heavy, it isn't feasible in many situations. Tile can also be installed with adhesive on two opposing layers of plywood (the existing subfloor with one additional layer screwed to it) or over cement backer board.

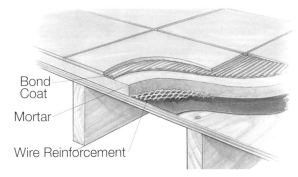

Bond Coat
Mortar
Wire Reinforcement

TILE OVER MORTAR

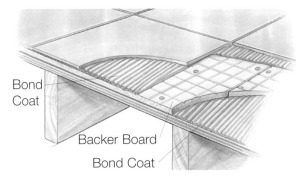

Bond Coat
Backer Board
Bond Coat

TILE OVER CEMENT BACKER BOARD

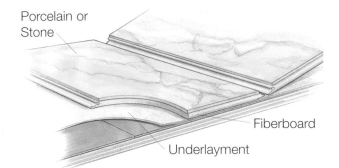

Porcelain or Stone
Fiberboard
Underlayment

FLOATING TILE PLANKS

grout joints

Joint widths can range in size from $\frac{1}{16}$ to $\frac{1}{2}$ inch or more. Large joints work best with large tiles and give a more rustic look. Small joints allow the tiled surface to look more like an unbroken plane and are best with contemporary styles, although some large polished marble tiles are set with a small joint for a classic effect.

Aside from aesthetic considerations, joints allow the installer to accommodate variances in tile size. If the difference between the largest tile in the carton and smallest is $\frac{1}{8}$ inch, installers will want at least a $\frac{1}{4}$-inch joint to accommodate them. Otherwise, the variations will be

bright idea

colored grout

Use colored grout to create either contrasting or blended effects. Dark colored grout, such as gray, will help hide staining. Or use an cpoxy grout: it's much easier to clean.

tiles that click

A new tiling system allows do-it-yourselfers to install a porcelain tile floor without mortar, backer board, or adhesives. It's also lighter than conventional tile installations and raises the existing floor only about ½ inch. You will, however, still have to learn to cut tile with a wet saw.

Cover subfloor with the underlayment recommended by thc manufacturer.

Click 12 x 24-in.-tile planks together, starting at the center of the room. Cut tiles to fit last rows with a wel saw that you can rent at most home centers.

Apply grout to joints, allow to set up, and wipe away excess.

The final result looks no different than tile installed on backer board or a mortar bed.

noticeable in the final result. Width of joint also allows the installer to accommodate slight height differences between tiles by sloping the grout.

Grout is used to fill the joints between tiles. It comes in several types and many colors. Common types include sanded (with fine sand mixed in) and nonsanded. Use sanded grout for joints ⅛ inch and wider. Use nonsanded grout for joint less than ⅛ inch wide. Epoxy grouts are fast becoming the standard because they are much easier to clean.

4

S ynthetic flooring wasn't developed until 60 or 70 years ago, but since then it has dominated the flooring market. Vinyl tile and sheet flooring and synthetic-fiber carpeting are the leaders. Laminate flooring, a more recent flooring innovation, has grabbed a significant share of the market as well. The popularity of synthetic floors is largely due to convenience and cost. They are easy to install and maintain. While it's not difficult to tell synthetics from the real stone, wood, tile, and fibers they mimic, many homeowners find that the lower installed cost outweighs aesthetic concerns.

Synthetic Flooring

❚ laminates ❚ sheet vinyl ❚ vinyl tiles ❚
❚ rubber and polypropylene ❚
❚ wall-to-wall carpeting ❚

Laminate flooring is shown here in a hickory look. Especially suitable for remodeling due to its thinness and ease of installation, more laminate is installed today than real-wood flooring.

laminate floors

ABOVE Laminate in a slate style is far easier to install and costs much less than the real thing.

RIGHT There won't be splinters from this barn board, a reproduction embedded in tough resin.

Popular in Europe for decades, laminate flooring has caught on in the United States and is now available from several dozen manufacturers. Not unlike laminate countertops—but much harder—laminate floors consist of protective and decorative layers that are bonded to a dense fiberboard core and backed with a moisture-resistant bottom layer. (See the illustration on page 89.) The decorative layer is a photo printed on paper and embedded in resin. Most styles imitate wood in every imaginable species and configuration. The top-of-the-line products are beveled and embossed so the spaces between boards and the graining look remarkably realistic. Other styles imitate tile or stone.

Contributing to the popularity of laminate is its ease of installation. No need to nail or staple it to a subfloor—it floats (rests on) the old floor. Nor does the floor below require a lot of prep. Unlike vinyl, laminate flooring will not telegraph minor subfloor imperfections to the surface. Available as planks or tiles, laminate flooring snaps together using various tongue-and-groove configurations. In the rare instance of a damaged plank, replacement is relatively easy. Laminate flooring's main disadvantage is that, unlike solid and engineered wood products, it cannot be refinished. Also, it can produce a hollow sound when you walk on it. Several manufacturers, however, apply a sound-inhibiting layer to the back. For those that don't, the recommendation is to install a foam underlayment.

ABOVE This family room's hickory-inspired laminate plank will stand up to all the abuse kids can deliver.

BELOW LEFT Laminate planks can produce the sophisticated look of herringbone strip flooring.

BELOW RIGHT Laminate planks are also available in dark stains, with beveled edges and grain textures.

LEFT Wood and tile are not the only styles produced in laminate. In this sun room, laminate imitates brick.

BELOW LEFT In this family room, laminate looks like cork.

BELOW RIGHT The bamboo look, in laminate, graces this breakfast nook.

I I I I I I I I I I I I I I I I I change a floor in a weekend I I I I I I I I I I I I I I I I

inside laminates

Laminate floors have moisture protection on top and on the bottom, allowing them to be used in moisture-prone areas—such as basements, kitchens, and baths. Regardless, care must be taken with their installation—including doing a moisture test, acclimating the flooring prior to installation, and using vapor barriers and sealants.

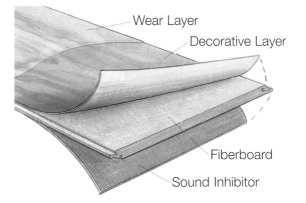

Wear Layer

Decorative Layer

Fiberboard

Sound Inhibitor

ABOVE Laminates in tile styles, such as this stone look, are among the most lifelike. Unlike many natural wood patterns, it's more difficult to detect the pattern repetitions.

RIGHT Laminate floors have a tough finish and, unlike wood, do not change color over time. Once the top layer wears, however, it cannot be refinished.

sheet vinyl

S sheet vinyl flooring is a fast way to a new floor. It installs in wide sheets, 6 to 15 feet wide, minimizing seams and joints that can collect dirt. It's also easy to clean—you don't have to worry about it being damaged by water. Most residential products consist of several layers, including a backing, a core layer, a decorative layer, and one or two protective layers. The decorative layer is either printed in multiple colors or created with inlaid colored vinyl chips that are bonded with heat and pressure. Luxury-grade sheet vinyl flooring is available with deep, random texturing, making imitations of natural material more realistic looking than ever before. In commercial grades, sheet vinyl flooring is often homogeneous (the color and pattern go all the way through the product), making nicks and gouges less likely to show. It can be used in homes to create distinctive floors. As quality can vary greatly with sheet vinyl flooring, keep in mind that the thicker the clear wear layer (measured in mil, or thousandths of an inch) the more durable the product. Sheet vinyl flooring is best installed by a professional. If you decide to install it yourself, some manufacturers take the pressure off by promising to send you new material if you make a mistake.

LEFT AND BELOW LEFT
Sheet vinyl flooring is now
available in sophisticated patterns, such as these embossed
leaf and mosaic designs.

ABOVE Imitation wood looks
surprisingly real with vinyl's
new matte finishes.

ABOVE RIGHT The granite-like
texture of this kitchen's sheet
flooring will hide crumbs until
you have a chance to sweep.

bright idea
coordination

Choose a sheet floor-
ing that coordinates
with your countertop;
this concrete-like
vinyl matches up
with the concrete
countertop.

types of **s**heet **v**inyl **f**looring

Sheet vinyl flooring is called a resilient flooring because at its core, the vinyl layer "gives" slightly. Inlaid vinyl uses tiny chips to create textures and patterns. Rotogravure-printed vinyl relies on photography. It does the best job of imitating wood and stone. Cushioned sheets, such as the fiberglass-reinforced products, offer the most resilience. For more on the latter, see "Fiberglass-Reinforced Vinyl" on the opposite page.

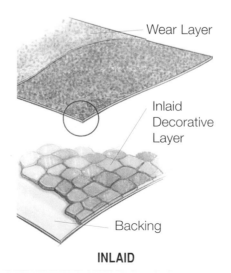

Wear Layer

Inlaid Decorative Layer

Backing

INLAID

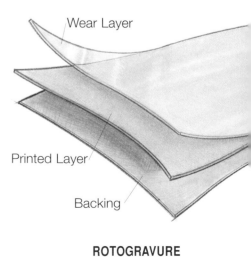

Wear Layer

Printed Layer

Backing

ROTOGRAVURE

fiberglass-**r**einforced **v**inyl

Sheet vinyl flooring reinforced with fiberglass has been introduced to the United States in the last few years. Vinyl's answer to glueless laminates, it has been popular for over a decade in Europe, where it has largely supplanted traditional sheet vinyl flooring. Fiberglass-reinforced vinyl is extremely pliable and easy to install. Just cut it to size, and lay it down. It won't curl, contract, or expand with temperature or humidity, so it doesn't need to be glued or fastened around the perimeter. This flooring has a relatively thick foam core (varies with quality), making it more resilient and comfortable to walk on than most other vinyl floors. It is also easy to clean and durable, making it ideal for children's rooms and recreation rooms. Manufacturers tout this product as flooring you can change every time you repaint or redecorate. Just roll it up and roll down a new pattern. Fiberglass-reinforced vinyl is available in rolls of about 13 feet. If your room is wider, the seam can be chemically bonded.

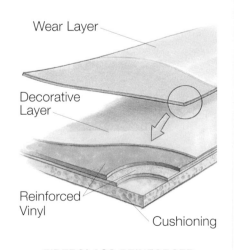

Wear Layer

Decorative
Layer

Reinforced
Vinyl

Cushioning

FIBERGLASS-REINFORCED

**OPPOSITE
AND ABOVE**
Shine has lost its luster in flooring fashions. Consequently, new styles from manufacturers sport matte and satin finishes.

∎

RIGHT Fiberglass-reinforced vinyl is more supple than traditional sheet vinyl. And it won't curl at room perimeters, even if it's left unfastened.

vinyl tiles

Vinyl tiles come in three types: solid vinyl, printed vinyl, and vinyl composite. Solid tiles have a less plastic, more natural look and are made by molding or rolling the vinyl resins and fillers to the desired shape. The appealing patterns are often abstract. Printed vinyl tiles are made using a layering process similar to that of residential sheet flooring. They come in a greater variety of color and pattern than other types of vinyl flooring, including very realistic-looking stone and wood, and are easy to install. Many, in fact, come with a self-stick backing, eliminating the need to apply adhesive. Vinyl composite tile (VCT) has mineral-dust filler added to the vinyl resins. As a consequence, it is extremely hard-wearing and is often used commercially. It comes in an interesting palette of solid colors and terrazzo-like patterns. The colors of both VCT and solid-vinyl types go through the tile, making nicks and wear less likely to show. Printed vinyl tiles usually come with a tough protective layer, making them easier to clean and care for than other types of vinyl tile that often require stripping and polishing. The latter are more durable and longer lasting, however.

LEFT Marblized vinyl gives this bath a classic look but is a lot more comfortable for bare feet.

ABOVE Vinyl tile lends itself to custom flooring. For example, in a large kitchen you can combine four solid-color vinyl tiles to create big, bold squares.

RIGHT In tight quarters, go with a smaller grid, as shown, or with a simple textured pattern.

bright idea

Upscale

Use vinyl tiles in a
large-scale pattern
to bring a big space
down to size.

I I I I I I I I I I I I I I use vinyl to advantage I I I I I I I I I I I I I I I

ABOVE Multihued, floor-softening textures in vinyl tile are often easier to color-match with cabinetry than natural wood and tiles.

LEFT Photographic reproduction and embossing combine to create convincing vinyl stone tiles.

BELOW Dark-stained faux burl wood planking, in vinyl, is at home in this colonial kitchen and the dining area beyond.

bright idea
rural chic

Combine plank and square tiles to create custom looks, such as this stone and wood combo.

ABOVE Once used mostly to imitate ceramic tile, new vinyl introductions are predominantly wood or stone imitations, as with these examples.

LEFT Vinyl is an ideal material for entryways and mudrooms, as shown with this European farmhouse scheme.

LEFT Polypropylene tiles, with slip-resistant textures, are a good solution for garage and basement workshops and laundries.

BELOW LEFT These tiles interlock and float but stand up to the weight of automobiles and stationary power tools.

BELOW Rubber tiles in bright colors and a "coin" texture are a practical and cheerful flooring solution for kitchens, laundries, and weight rooms.

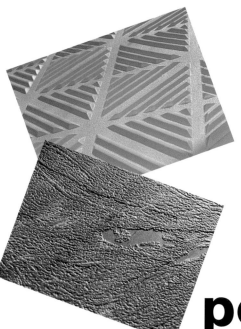

LEFT AND BELOW Rubber tile styles range from waffle textures and bright colors (top) to subdued marbled patterns reminiscent of tiles from the past (bottom).

rubber and polypropylene

Rubber flooring is used mostly in commercial settings, such as fitness centers and retail stores, but it is becoming more popular in homes as well. Rubber is very resilient, stain- and water-resistant, and durable. It also has good soundproofing qualities and offers superior traction. Rubber makes a good choice for basement stairs, garages, home gyms, laundries, home offices, and workshops. It is also supple and flexible enough to "self-cove" a room—create a baseboard and floor all in one piece.

Rubber flooring is available in 12-, 18-, and 36-inch-square tiles, or in long sheets. Some types of rubber tile are interlocking, making for an adhesive-free installation; others are not. Colors and patterns are plentiful, ranging from familiar studded and diamond patterns, to terrazzo-like products where virgin rubber, recycled tires, and other rubber consumer products are shredded and fused together. Cork and rubber are sometimes combined to create flooring with the benefits of both: comfort, an earthy look, sound reduction, and slip resistance.

Polypropylene tiles are made from dense plastic resins that are resistant to oil, grease, and antifreeze, making them another good option if you're looking to upgrade your garage floor. They can also withstand heavy loads, making flow-through (perforated) floors possible (in case you want to direct melt-off to a drain in your floor). These interlocking tiles can be installed directly over a level concrete floor in the garage or basement laundry. They are also easy to clean, and you can take them with you if you move.

Wall-to-wall carpeting is the most popular floor covering in the United States. It's quiet, warm, and comfortable when you walk or sit on it; isn't slippery; doesn't hurt as much if you fall; and comes in styles and colors to suit any decor. Best of all, it can cover a plywood subfloor at less cost than that of any other floor covering. While some homeowners see wall-to-wall carpeting as a temporary solution while saving up for wood or tile, others invest in top-quality products and plan to enjoy them for many years.

When shopping for carpeting, know your fibers. Each one has its strengths and weaknesses. Acrylics, for example, are usually the most expensive

wall-to-wall carpeting

because they look like wool and resist staining, crushing, and fading. They do not hold up to heavy traffic, however, making them more suitable for bedrooms and other private areas in the home. Nylon, the first synthetic fiber for carpeting, remains the favorite among homeowners due to its durability and steadfast colors. Its resilient fibers stand up well to furniture and traffic but can be damaged if exposed to sunlight for long periods. Polyesters are less durable and resilient than nylon but less costly, too. They are available in a wide range of deep vivid colors that resist fading and staining. Olefin (polypropylene) is commonly used in commercial and indoor-outdoor applications due to its low cost and superior stain resistance.

OPPOSITE Elegant, restrained patterns distinguish today's wall-to-wall carpeting.

ABOVE Shag carpeting is back, but new thicker pile gives it a plushier feel and makes it less likely to flatten.

LEFT Choose a compact loop pile and moistureproof padding for a child's room.

RIGHT Wall-to-wall synthetic carpeting, although affected by higher oil prices, remains one of the least-expensive flooring solutions. At the same time, it's one of the most comfortable and versatile—at home in both formal and casual settings.

carpet textures

Carpet texture is based largely on whether the pile (yarn surface) is cut or not. With cut pile, the loops of a woven or tufted carpet are trimmed to create a smooth brush-like pile. Velvet, plush, and saxony are examples of smooth cut-pile carpeting and are well-suited for use in formal areas. The same method is used to produce textured, shag, and frieze carpeting. Loop-pile carpets, on the other hand, leave the yarn loops uncut. Berber, cable, and multilevel-loop styles are all loop-pile carpets. They hold up well to traffic, are easy to clean, and hide footprints extremely well.

Plush or Velvet

Saxony

Friezé or Twist

Loop Pile

Cut and Loop

Textured

tufted **v**ersus **w**oven **c**arpets

For centuries, rugs and carpets were woven. In the beginning of the twentieth century, tufted rugs were pioneered in Dalton, Georgia. Today, tufted products are the most prevalent in the wall-to-wall category due to cost, but they cannot match the beauty or durability of woven carpet. Tufted carpet technology, however, continues to improve and can now be used to create intricate patterns not possible in the past.

In a tufted carpet, the yarn is inserted through a mesh backing (visible at left) and held in place with adhesive. Once the tufting is complete, a second mesh backing (above) is adhered to the first for stability.

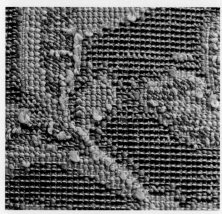

Woven carpets are made with various types of weaving processes, each with a distinct character. In general, strong warp (vertical) yarns are interwoven with softer weft (horizontal) yarns. With a woven carpet, you can often see the surface design on the back (above).

fiber **f**acts

1 Berber-style carpets, originally inspired by coarse-textured carpets that were handcrafted in northern Africa, are now available in myriad styles.

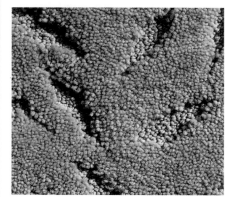

2 Tufted carpet manufacturers create interesting "sculpted" patterns by combining short loops and cut pile.

3 One of several specialty weaves, Axminster produces patterns with beautiful clarity.

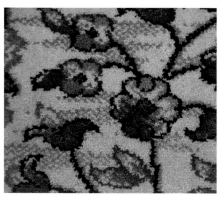

4 Although the majority of wall-to-wall carpeting is of the tufted variety, it is also available in woven styles, such as this Wilton weave.

BELOW Carpeting is the perfect surface for families that spend as much time lounging on the floor as they do on couches and chairs. To make the floor really inviting, you can install a radiant-floor heating system under the carpet, but choose your padding carefully. Slab-rubber or synthetic-fiber carpet cushions are best at allowing heat to penetrate the room.

OPPOSITE TOP Today's "jute" paddings are made from synthetic fibers. They are available in many different weights to handle low, medium, and high-traffic situations. Install padding that is waterproof to preserve your wood floors underneath the carpet.

OPPOSITE BOTTOM Carpet tiles have a light adhesive backing and come in dozens of textures and colors. Create area rugs or wall-to-wall carpets of any size. A big advantage to carpet tiles: you can replace stained or damaged tiles quickly and easily.

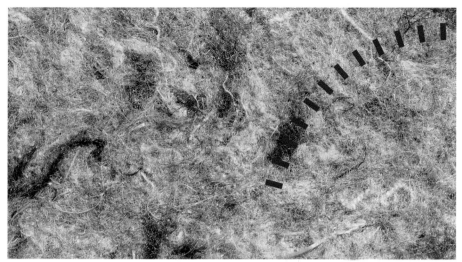

Upgrade

Carpet dealers often throw in the padding with your purchase. Instead, upgrade to a better padding, such as slab rubber or frothed foam. They will both improve carpet performance and prevent spills from leaking through to the flooring below.

dual **p**urpose

Padding is generally recommended for use under carpeting. Available in various thicknesses, from ¼ to ⁷⁄₁₆ inch, it serves two purposes: first, it makes carpeting more resilient and consequently more comfortable for walking. Second, it helps to preserve the carpet by preventing fibers from being crushed. From good to best, padding types include rebond (a high density foam), slab rubber, jute or fiber (made from jute or synthetic fiber), and frothed foam (high-density polyurethane).

5

Kitchens, bathrooms, and laundries are arguably the hardest-working rooms in the home and consequently need the toughest floors. In kitchens we spill, splatter, feed pets, collect trash, and, for those with back doors, track in mud. In bathrooms, we splash, steam, groom, and preen, often in bare feet. In laundries, we add strong detergents and bleaches to the mix. In all three spaccs, the floors must be extra slip-resistant, comfortable, and easy to make sparkling clean. On top of it all, these floors must look great—especially in kitchens and baths, where we've invested the most money.

Where It Gets Wet

I kitchens I baths I
I laundries I

The mosaic look and feel of this sheet vinyl floor is equally at home in a large or small bath. The texture provides good traction, and the absence of seams means fewer moisture problems.

ABOVE Cork is a superb flooring for kitchens. It gets top grades for comfort, safety, moisture resistance, and beauty.

LEFT Laminates (here in a slate reproduction close-up) are generally more moisture- and impact-resistant than wood or bamboo, making them a good choice for kitchens.

OPPOSITE Real slate flooring is a gorgeous material. Place mats at work stations to make it easier on your legs. In this kitchen, slate does double duty as a countertop.

The most practical choice for a kitchen floor is a resilient vinyl tile or sheet vinyl flooring. It's easy on the feet, easy to install, easy to keep clean, and easy on the wallet. Many of the new styles are also easy on the eyes. It addition, it's resistant to slips and stains, and you'll break far fewer glasses and dishes on it than on ceramic tile or stone. Vinyl comes in more styles than any other type of flooring, so you're almost certain to find a product that suits your decor.

kitchens

Laminate, bamboo, linoleum, cork, tile, and wood are good alternatives, but each has its drawbacks. Laminate, for example, is difficult to repair and cannot be refinished. Linoleum and cork are relatively costly. Tile is hard and cold. And wood and bamboo will require vigilance around wet areas, such as the sink, dishwasher, and pet's water bowl. On the other hand, each of these materials has a look and feel that may simply appeal to you more than vinyl.

There are a number of things you can do to get the most from your kitchen-floor investment. Keep a large fiber mat in front of any entrance from the outdoors. Coconut husk fibers, at least ⅜ inch deep, do a good job. Use nonslip mats in front of areas prone to drips, splatters, and spills, such as at the range, sink, and dishwasher. Sweep the floor every evening after dinner, and clean it regularly according to the manufacturer's directions. A slippered-feet policy in the home will make any floor last years longer.

I I I I I I match floor to decor I I I I I I I I I I I I I I I I I I I I I I I I I I I I I I I

upgrading to **w**ood

Despite some drawbacks, many homeowners want the country look of wood in their kitchen (right). If you're among them, engineered wood products are your best choice. They are available in many species and stain colors. Thinner planks make it easier to approximate the heights of adjacent floors, and engineered products withstand moisture remarkably well. Installation is easier thanks to glued and glueless (floated) options, although some products require nails or staples.

As is the case with most flooring, the subfloor must be carefully prepared. If it's not level, the new wood floor won't be either. Voids must be filled and loose boards screwed down, or the floor will squeak later. If your subfloor has minor humps or if the plywood subflooring is slightly raised around the edges, you may rent an edger (a powerful sanding machine) to level it. Minor dips may be shimmed with 30-pound roofing felt. Major dips may need to be shimmed with plywood and feathered to meet the existing subfloor—a job best left to a pro.

OPPOSITE Vinyl styles have become sophisticated enough to fit in perfectly with today's minimalist decorating tastes.

OPPOSITE FAR LEFT This custom linoleum floor evokes the first half of the last century.

LEFT This natural ceramic tile has a handmade look and gives this kitchen an earthy footing.

RIGHT More laminate, as shown, is installed in the United States than solid and engineered-wood flooring combined.

bathrooms

ABOVE New vinyl styles, such as this sheet product with a subtle floral pattern, are suitable for even the most luxurious master suite.

RIGHT Rectangular ceramic tiles layed in a brick pattern are the perfect play for this master bath.

OPPOSITE The soapstone tiles used in this bathroom have a more refined look than slate. They are also extremely durable and resist acids.

Vinyl is the most popular bathroom flooring for many of the same reasons it performs so well in kitchens. But unlike kitchens, baths can be divided into two types: public (those that will be frequented by both family members and visitors, often wearing shoes) and private (family only).

With private baths, it's OK to indulge yourself. Go ahead and splurge on a more sensuous material for the room where you peel off clothing every day. Wood, ceramic, or porcelain tile, stone, and even wall-to-wall carpeting, in the right circumstance, offer appealing alternatives to the practicality of vinyl.

In public bathrooms and powder rooms, economize with a good-quality vinyl. Hands down, it beats other popular choices, such as tile and stone, for safety, comfort, and maintenance. Laminate, in either wood or tile styles, is an excellent choice as well, especially for remodeling. Installed, it does not raise the existing floor much, so making transitions to adjacent hallways is easier. In addition, laminates are durable and easy to keep clean. The only area where it falls short of vinyl is with moisture. You can't leave standing water on it for long, or it may infiltrate the fiberboard core and cause it to expand. Similarly, it's important to caulk gaps along the walls, tub, and other fixtures to prevent water infiltration around the perimeter of the room.

RIGHT This sleek contemporary bath has the black and white floor pattern mirrored on the ceiling.

BELOW Not all tile looks like stone. Bright colors are making a comeback. Opt for a matte finish for a safer footing.

OPPOSITE TOP Sheet vinyl flooring in a reptilian skin texture makes this bath floor ultra chic and most practical.

avoid damage to new floors

Some floors installed with adhesive, such as ceramic tile, often require special care when brand new. Except for removing stray smudges of adhesive, do not wash the floor for the period recommended by the manufacturer. Moisture may affect the bond. Keep foot traffic to a minimum as well. Wait 24 hours before rolling appliances back into place. And when you do, clean the floor well and put down a ¼-inch sheet of hardboard or plywood for protection as you roll them into place.

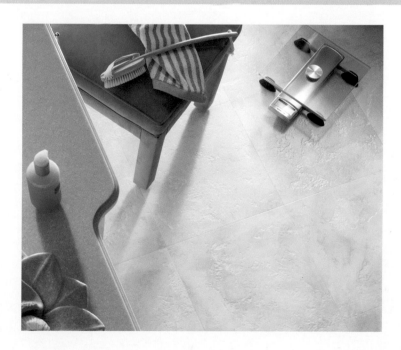

ABOVE Tile manufacturers often create lines of coordinated wall and floor tiles. Here, the subtle color of the glazed porcelain floor tile blends beautifully with that of the glass tile on the walls.

RIGHT Stone in a shard pattern (tumbled for softened edges) makes a smashing bath. The interlocking tiles come preassembled on a mesh backing.

BELOW Pebble patterns are also available for floors. Grout between the rounded stones just as you do with tile.

radiant heat

Several manufacturers now market radiant-floor-heating systems that will make early-morning kitchen and bath floors more comfortable. Typically electrically and thermostatically controlled, the ⅛-inch-thick heating membrane is installed between the subfloor and finished floor. It is most often used under ceramic tiles and stone but can also be used beneath engineered wood and laminate floors. Check with your finished floor manufacturer to find out the maximum temperature for your floor. Many product manuals warn against temperatures above 85°F.

▌ First, apply thinset compound to the subfloor with the notched trowel recommended by the manufacturer.

▌ Next, roll out the heating mats. They are typically about ⅛ inch thick, with electrical resistance wire encased between two layers. Some products are cables backed with mesh.

▌ For ceramic tile, apply adhesive directly over the mats. Have a certified electrician make the final connection to a dedicated circuit.

The combination of clutter, chemicals, dirt, and moisture should make slip resistance and easy cleanup your top criteria when choosing laundry-room flooring. If you spend time on your feet folding and sorting in the laundry, resiliency is a factor as well. For basement laundries not subject to groundwater problems, a slip-resistant vinyl tile or sheet flooring is a smart choice. To install it, first you may have to put down a plywood subfloor in the laun-

laundries

dry area. A concrete floor, colored or textured, will be easier to clean and more pleasant to look at than a raw concrete floor. It will also be less likely to peel than painted concrete floors, even those coated with an epoxy. Rubber matting in the areas where you stand will make the concrete easier on your legs. If your base-ment has moisture problems, consider a removable interlocking tile in rubber or polypropy-lene. There are also interlocking bamboo and wood tiles, if you prefer the look and feel of wood. They consist of ½-inch planks attached to a plastic base. If your laundry is on the main level, vinyl, rubber, cork, and matte-finished porcelain or ceramic tile are all excellent choices.

LEFT Lightly textured vinyl sheet flooring pro-vides a no-seam, easy-to-clean, economical laundry flooring surface.

OPPOSITE TOP Slate stands up to the demands of this combi-nation laundry and mudroom.

OPPOSITE BOTTOM LEFT Lami-nate flooring, styled to look like stone, is easy to keep dirt free and is unaffected by detergent.

OPPOSITE BOTTOM RIGHT Rectangular tiles with a brushed glaze and natu-ral imperfections make a rustic but serviceable laundry floor.

6

In the rooms where we relax, play, entertain, and sleep, it's fun to let your floors show off your personal style. Yes, they've still got to be practical—but unlike more demanding spaces, such as such as kitchens, baths, and foyers, the emphasis can shift to self-expression. If you want to make an environmental statement, choose flooring made from renewable resources. If you love to travel, let your flooring be inspired by the ideas you've seen. Love nature? Make connections to the outdoors. With the explosion of flooring styles in the last decade, there's plenty from which to choose.

Get Personal

living and dining rooms ▮ bedrooms
▮ family rooms ▮ recreation rooms ▮
▮ hobby and craft rooms ▮

Think of the home—especially living rooms, dining rooms, and bedrooms—as a blank canvas upon which you can express yourself. Think of floor coverings as the base color.

living and dining rooms

The living room is traditionally a place to entertain visitors. As such, it is the perfect room in which to make a personal statement. Carpeting—whether wall-to-wall, area rugs, or both—is hard to beat because it can evoke so many different periods and places. In a colonial setting, you can opt for anything from bright, bold hooked rugs with a handcrafted look to a resplendent Oriental design. On the other end of the spectrum, you can find designs inspired by Miro and Mondrian. A European look favors layering small area rugs over a large one. Whatever you choose, tempt guests to sit on the floor with carpet that's thick, plush, and well-padded.

Wood in an engineered or solid product is a versatile alternative to carpeting. You can aim for a laid-back, rustic Western look; a dark, stately, polished Beacon Hill presentation; or a cooly elegant Scandinavian feel in blonde, natural, or off-white tones. It is also the ideal surface for showing off your prized area rugs.

Wood or laminate is a good choice for a dining area. Chairs slide easily (with felt pads under the legs), and cleanup is a snap. You may want to avoid carpeting under the dining room table, even if it is stain resistant, or you'll spend a lot of time worrying about food and drink stains. But if carpet is your heart's desire, consider a dark color so stains won't show as readily. Or, use replaceable carpet tiles. The dining room is also the ideal candidate for a custom floor, a place where you and your guests can admire it while savoring your latest culinary creation. Cork, linoleum, and tile offer limitless possibilities.

LEFT Natural hickory planks, coated with a durable factory finish, underpin this contemporary dining area.

OPPOSITE TOP Naturally dark wood species, often from Brazil, or dark-stained woods set an established, formal tone—as in this eclectic-style living room.

OPPOSITE BOTTOM LEFT The wild grain patterns and distress marks contribute to the lodge-like looks of this living room.

OPPOSITE BOTTOM RIGHT This Brazilian ironwood's natural color makes staining unnecessary. It's an engineered product, helping to conserve this not very renewable wood species.

ABOVE LEFT Wall-to-wall carpeting simplifies and softens the look of any room.

ABOVE RIGHT Luxury sheet vinyl flooring, here in a large-tile style, is perfect for a combination dining and living room.

RIGHT Linoleum lets you express yourself with color and shape, as in this modern living room.

OPPOSITE FAR RIGHT Oak remains the most popular choice for wood floors; the one pictured here has a red stain that accentuates its natural warm country tones.

disappearing **w**alls

The lines between dining rooms, living rooms, family rooms, and kitchens continue to blur, according to the American Institute of Architects' (AIA) recent home-design trends survey. Open, informal spaces continue to increase, along with wider hallways and more single-floor layouts. This can pose some real design dilemmas, because the floors in several "rooms" can all be seen at once. One solution is to use a wall substitute to break up a wide expanse of flooring, such as the columns and half-wall in the photo at right. Another approach is to use several complementary flooring types to make large open-space plans more coherent and intimate. However, avoid chopping up small open-space plans with different flooring materials.

III **personality and function** IIIIIIIIIIIIIIIIIIIIII

RIGHT A bordered sisal rug over a wood floor blends with the outdoors theme of this living room.

BELOW LEFT A deep-toned engineered oak floor serves as an anchoring element in this living space, allowing other features—millwork and a favorite painting—to shine.

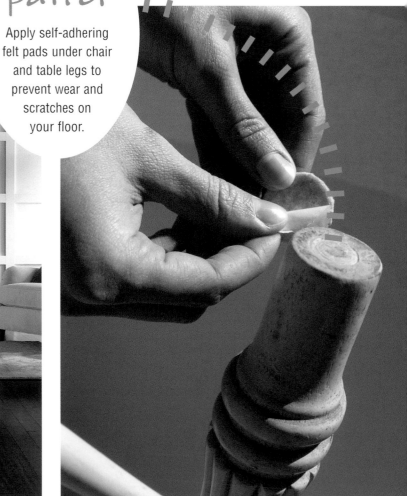

bright idea

scratch patrol

Apply self-adhering felt pads under chair and table legs to prevent wear and scratches on your floor.

RIGHT If you don't want to agonize over scratches and spills, especially with kids around, a fiberglass-reinforced vinyl floor in a sophisticated print could be just right for your dining room. It will keep down the din, too.

| | | | | | | | lose your design inhibitions here | | | | | | | | | | | | | | | | | | | |

B edrooms are sanctuaries where you can close the door on the world to relax and sleep. Because they are lightly trafficked, usually in stocking feet, you can indulge yourself with any flooring that gives you a sense of well-being. Carpeting and area rugs, as previously discussed, are two of the most comfortable types of flooring. They also permit a wide range of self-expression. For the sensualist, a thick, nubby Berber or deep plush pile is hard to resist. Seeking simplicity and inner peace? Consider a subtly beautiful carpet made of paper. Stuck in the '70s? Shag rugs are back with some of their original shagadelic exuberance, as well as more conservative designs.

bedrooms

Kid-themed rugs for children's rooms range from educational—numbers, shapes, and letters—to youth-inspired solid colors, such as blueberry pie and fire-engine red. Keep in mind that despite our best efforts, kids do grow up quickly—so avoid babyish themes, as they will soon be obsolete. Select a kid's room carpet that's comfortable to sit and lie on and is stain-resistant.

LEFT Wood flooring, such as this Tauari engineered plank, is a popular choice in the bedroom for allergy sufferers.

OPPOSITE FAR LEFT This distinctive leaf-patterned sheet vinyl may be just the thing for a vacation-home bedroom or for a bedroom that's filled with plants.

LEFT In private rooms, let go of your decorating inhibitions, as this homeowner did with a splatter-and-blob carpet in primary colors.

RIGHT The black walnut graining of the laminate adds drama to the clean look of this bedroom, which was done in neutrals and whites.

family rooms

Family rooms often serve many purposes and many family members, so self-expression may turn to group expression here. Such rooms may be where youngsters play with trucks and building blocks, teens kick back to watch a movie, family members build models, sew, or draw—or all of the above. It's not uncommon to find stereo systems and video game consoles in today's family room.

With all of that activity and noise, sound-muffling wall-to-wall carpeting would be a good choice. A nylon fiber in a sisal or textured loop style, for example, wears well, resists staining and fading, and is comfortable. Place thick, cushioned area rugs where family members may sprawl on the floor to play games or watch TV.

If your family's favorite pursuits tend to be a little too messy for wall-to-wall carpeting (crayons, finger paint, and pizza parties), consider tiles in ceramic or porcelain, wood, cork, or laminate. Place well-padded area rugs as needed for comfort. They can be easily rolled out of the way when the paint starts to fly and can be removed for cleaning.

OPPOSITE BOTTOM LEFT
Wall-to-wall carpeting is available in wool as well as synthetics, with lots of styles from which to choose. Prices are more competitive with synthetics, as oil prices rise.

OPPOSITE BOTTOM RIGHT Engineered walnut flooring is exquisite in this contemporary media room.

LEFT AND BELOW If you have young children, a hard-wearing sheet vinyl in a lively pattern may be the answer.

BOTTOM LEFT If you want the feel of an old floor, loaded with dents and gauges, get a head start with this distressed-pine flooring. It comes preoiled, so it does not need finishing.

recreation rooms

P ing pong, pool, table soccer, treadmills, and free weights are just a sampling of what floors in recreation rooms might have to handle. If the room is in the basement, consider a custom decorative concrete floor or polymer-modified cement overlay. You can incorporate colors, textures—even the logos of your favorite sports teams. If moisture is not a problem in your basement, vinyl, engineered wood, and laminate are durable alternatives. All three can be installed directly over a level concrete floor or on a raised subfloor with the recommended vapor barriers and padding. If your recreation room isn't in the basement and you want to hold the noise down, cork, rubber sheet, rubber tile, or laminate (with protective rubber mats in the weights area) would make good alternatives.

OPPOSITE Wall-to-wall nylon-fiber carpeting in a loop texture makes sense for recreation rooms where adults play.

ABOVE Vinyl is a great choice for a recreation room for active kids. This sheet product is fiberglass-reinforced and offers some degree of cushioning.

LEFT Traditional sheet vinyl flooring, such as this stone-tile imitation, is a good choice for a basement recreation room, as long as you have solved any moisture problems prior to installation.

RIGHT This stone-look sheet vinyl floor floats for quick and easy installation.

hobbies and crafts

Hobby and craft spaces tend to be very personal. By their nature, they are often opportunities for self-expression. They may include everything from sewing rooms to places for kids (or adults) to have fun with glue. As such, there are many possible flooring options. For messy hobbies, vinyl is a good option in either sheet or tile because it's easy to clean. You may prefer wood, however, for its beauty and feel. Even if it gets splattered, it hardly matters. After all, a hobby-room floor is not expected to be perfect. A painted wood floor is a nice alternative. It can be renewed easily with a fresh coat. For less messy pursuits, such as model railroading or sewing, cork is ideal because it's easy on the legs for hobbyists who need to stand a lot; quiet; and a great insulator. Hobbies such as pottery making and plant growing can be quite messy and abrasive to floors, in which case a ceramic floor is the best choice.

OPPOSITE BOTTOM Bamboo can be layed with cork or other sound-dampening underlayment for a charming music room floor. This one has a hand-scraped look.

LEFT Vinyl in sheet or tile is an ideal choice for rooms with mess potential. This luxury vinyl tile is not only functional but beautiful, too. Its heavy texture hides the drips and spills.

ABOVE Keep scale in mind when making models as well as when choosing floor patterns. In this small model-maker's retreat, 3-in. tiles were just right.

bright idea

floors first

In an artist's studio, paint the floor before turning to your canvases. It can be renewed easily with an occasional recoating.

ABOVE An artist's studio floor is as critical for its functionality as it is for how it looks and feels.

LEFT Laminate is also a good choice for crafts rooms and art studios. The hard, impervious finish makes cleaning up spills easy here.

OPPOSITE If growing plants is your passion, opt for a floor that shrugs off soil and sand, such as this slate floor.

bright idea

shake it up

Add a wiggle to your floor with wide, irregular grout lines, as shown here.

W hen you're choosing flooring for heavy-use areas, you can select an economy-grade carpet or vinyl, opt for a highly durable material that's not going to wear regardless of the traffic, or compromise with a "better" grade of flooring and use protective mats or area rugs. The first approach has one thing going for it—it's cheap, at least in the short run. The last-forever approach will enhance your home and save you money in the long term but will require a bigger initial investment. The compromise approach is great for homeowners who want good looks and value.

Heavy-Duty Floors

| foyers and mudrooms |
| hallways and stairways |
| garages and basements |

Stone tile, as shown in this transition area, is a lifetime investment that will increase your home's value. Experts say they don't see the stone trend fading any time soon.

Flooring in foyers, mudrooms, and other entry areas takes more abuse than anywhere else. Vinyl, tile, and stone will stand up well to the water and dirt that inevitably gets tracked indoors. Of the three, stone will last the longest—probably the life of the house—but will require the most care. Tile will last nearly as long. Vinyl, depending upon the grade, comes with warranties of 10, 15, and even 20 years, and is the easiest to maintain.

Other flooring products, including wood and bamboo, will last decades in a foyer or entryway but will require more protection from moisture and dirt to keep them looking their best. Covering them with a washable rug when the weather is bad will help reduce maintenance. Just be sure to put a good-quality pad underneath to prevent the rug from sliding and to keep moisture and dirt from sifting through to the flooring below. Another good idea, if you go with wood or bamboo in a foyer or near an entrance, is to isolate it from surrounding wood floors with inset planks or tiles. This will allow you to refinish the flooring near the entrance without having to refinish the adjacent wood floors as well.

foyers and mudrooms

For foyers, keep in mind that you are setting the tone for the rest of your house. For a formal look, go with marble or a marble look-alike in vinyl or laminate. For rustic appeal, consider wood or terra-cotta tiles. For understated elegance, there's slate and terrazzo. Or go contemporary with rubber tile.

In mudrooms, on the other hand, the emphasis should be less on style and more on function. Their purpose is to keep dirt and water off the other floors in the rest of your home. As such, they should be equipped with storage for shoes, coats, and umbrellas—and with a floor that will stand up to abuse such as puddles from tracked-in snow or mud. Rubber, either sheet or tile, is a good choice. It is durable, slip-resistant, impervious to tracked-in salt, and nearly stain-proof. In addition, it's comfortable to walk on in stocking feet, thanks to its resiliency and insulating properties. Finally, its soundproofing qualities will work wonders with the clatter of shoes, book bags, and sports equipment as children come home from school or play. Another good choice is resilient vinyl sheet or vinyl tile that's been textured to improve slip-resistance. Ceramic tile, a perennial favorite for mudrooms, is often too slippery when wet. If you must have it, however, use 4 x 4-inch quarry tiles. The matte finish will reduce the chance for accidents, and the deep color won't show soil readily.

OPPOSITE TOP Ceramic and porcelain tiles can be used to support many decorating styles. In this foyer, the checkerboard creates a crisp, contemporary look.

OPPOSITE BOTTOM A warm color and lively border update this foyer.

RIGHT Tile in a diamond-and-square design, framed with dark grout, evokes a grand entrance from the Colonial era. The dark grout punches up the pattern.

bright idea

wow factor

Splurge on your foyer floor with a quality eye-popping stone or tile—and use a more budget-minded floor covering in the rest of the house.

┃┃┃┃┃┃┃ make a good first impression ┃┃┃┃┃┃┃┃┃┃┃┃┃┃┃┃┃┃┃┃┃┃┃┃

OPPOSITE Two sizes of square tiles, staggered, were used to create this intriguing pattern in porcelain tile.

ABOVE LEFT AND RIGHT Choose a foyer flooring material that will set the tone for the rest of your house, such as a casual stone or a more formal ceramic.

LEFT Slate is a popular choice for mudrooms for its beauty—and because it doesn't show the tracked-in dirt.

RIGHT Sheet vinyl flooring in a stone look is a practical and good-looking choice for this side entry hall.

RIGHT This spectacular linoleum hallway floor picks up colors from the paintings displayed on the walls.

OPPOSITE TOP Strand-woven is the hardest-wearing type of bamboo. It is suitable for high-traffic stairs and halls.

OPPOSITE BOTTOM Carpeted stairs and landings reduce household noise significantly. High yarn count and padding help to keep this carpet from wearing.

Hallways are often highly visible areas that concentrate traffic along a relatively narrow path. Consequently, you should select a quality flooring that complements or matches the surrounding floors, as well as one that wears well. A good choice is carpeting or wood with a runner placed over it to prevent excessive wear. Wood, whether it's solid or engineered, looks great with virtually any other flooring type. Carpeting and rugs will keep the noise down, which is especially important in hallways serving bedrooms.

Stairways may be thought of as hallways on an angle. Once again, they are often highly visible and highly trafficked architectural elements. Wood, bamboo, ceramic, and carpeting are, again, good choices. Although padding will help increase the wear life of stair

hallways and stairways

carpets, avoid thick padding at the tread nose. It can cause a misstep and fall. For utility stairs, such as those leading to the basement, consider adding ribbed rubber stair-tread covers to minimize any chance of slippage. They are available as tack-down, self-stick, or glue-on panels.

ABOVE Laminate flooring can look great and wear well on stairs. Use a sound-muffling underlayment, however, to minimize noise.

OPPOSITE TOP Runners in cheerful contemporary patterns brighten an otherwise dull and narrow hallway.

OPPOSITE BOTTOM Carry ceramic tile up the stairs using a matching bull nose at the edge of the tread.

carpet runners

Hallway and stair runners can really dress up what is often an overlooked space. They also reduce noise, add traction, cushion occasional slips, and take the brunt of wear and tear. Runners are available in natural and synthetic fibers, and the latter boast very dense pile of up to two million points (fibers) per square meter. Dense fiber (shown right) will resist soiling and wear better. Quality padding, no less than ¼ inch thick for stairs, will help keep your runners looking good for longer as well. Typically, runners come in widths from 2½ to 3 feet and lengths of up to 20 feet. You may choose to complement or match the pattern of a nearby area rug.

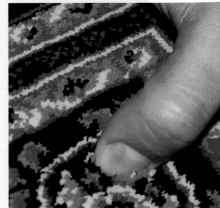

ABOVE Create giant "tiles" in your garage with acid staining, grooving, and a protective polyurethane finish coat.

OPPOSITE BOTTOM Opt for a granite finish with a polymer-modified cement overlay in a granite texture.

bright idea

spot remover

Large vinyl parking mats are an effective way to cover cracks. They also keep garage floors free of stains, salts, and sand. Pulled into the driveway, they can be hosed clean.

garages and basements

Not long ago, few people gave much thought to the flooring in basements and garages. Bare or perhaps painted concrete was the norm. With space in the home at a premium, however, more homeowners are converting basements to recreation rooms, workshops, and hobby or craft studios. Garages are getting more attention as well. Car enthusiasts want something nice under their prized autos. Woodworkers who use the garage as a workshop want something resilient and insulating underfoot.

Rubber and vinyl (in tiles or sheets) make ideal surfaces for basement workshops and studios. If you want something nicer than unfinished or cracked concrete as a floor, either an acid-stained concrete or a polymer-modified cement overlay would transform your garage into a showroom. Resurfacing with removable rubber or polyethylene tiles is a good garage-floor solution, too.

vent moisture away

▍ **Studs on the underside** of prefabricated subfloor tiles provide a ¼-inch space for venting away moisture.

▍ **The subfloor tiles have a layer** of oriented-strand board on top and fit together with a tongue-and-groove joint.

▍ **Plastic shims** allow you to level panels as you install them.

ABOVE Vinyl tile may be glued directly to a smooth, level concrete slab. More likely you will need to add a subfloor first, using a system such as the one described, left, or by traditional methods.

▍

RIGHT Floating floors, such as this engineered plank, can also be used for basement flooring.

8

Floors are rarely the focal point of a room. However, this need not be the case. Flooring can steal the show. One way is to design your own custom floor. Many flooring materials lend themselves to customization. Another approach is to enhance an otherwise plain floor with decorative accents, such as medallions and borders. You can design your own or buy them ready-made. Painted designs on floor cloths, carpet, or wood can also grab attention. Even concrete and stone flooring can be etched or sandblasted with the textures, patterns, or images you desire.

Special Effects

▮ custom designs ▮ borders ▮
▮ medallions ▮ mosaics ▮
▮ painted floors and floor cloths ▮

This painted compass rose looks like an inlay of marble, wood, and metal. The artist muted the wood grain and coloring of the surrounding floor to heighten the contrast.

Virtually every type of flooring allows some degree of customization. There are limitless possibilities, for example, with tile of all types (vinyl, stone, cork, and so forth). Create simple checkerboards and weaves or more sophisticated asymmetrical patterns. Some manufacturers offer interactive programs on their Web sites to help you visualize your design. Experienced flooring contractors and interior designers can also assist you.

Vinyl, cork, and linoleum sheet goods can also be cut and pieced together to create intriguing one-of-a-kind designs. Carpets can be custom-made as well, either by sewing together sections or by services that will duplicate just about any image you can imagine. Finally, paint can work wonders, even with the tightest of budgets. Use it to transform wood, tile, canvas, or carpet.

custom designs

OPPOSITE Mosaic borders and large field tiles are used here to create a giant windowpane pattern.

TOP Cork in a diagonal stripe helps to prevent the stone fireplace from becoming too dominant in this living room.

LEFT Contrasting maple strips and planks create a low-cost focal point in this formal entrance.

LEFT Use ceramic tiles to add color and define areas within open floor plans.

BELOW, ALL Use vinyl tiles the same way. They can underscore a kitchen island (left), frame a floor (center), or for a more daring look, form wide stripes (right).

OPPOSITE Here, vinyl tiles are used in a diagonal weave to create an eye-opening entry-way floor.

IIIII make flooring the focus IIIIIIIIIIIIIIIIIIIIIIIIIIIIIIIIIIIII

custom linoleum

1 **Make cardboard templates** of your floor design, and use them to mark cutting lines on the linoleum. Cut pieces with a utility knife and straightedge.

2 **Ensure a tight fit** with inserts, such as this diamond, by using the cutout as a template for tracing.

3 **Preassemble pieces** with tape to make the installation easier.

4 **Install the preassembled pieces** using the adhesive recommended by the manufacturer.

ABOVE An accent inspired by an African mask is the focal point for this dining room.

BELOW The designer incorporated a fiber doormat into this custom linoleum foyer floor.

OPPOSITE A premade border and custom "rug" stylize this sitting area.

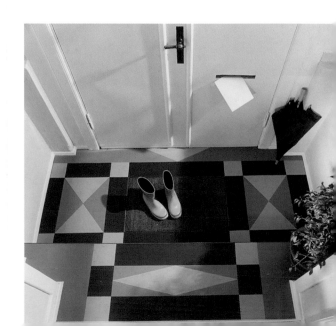

RIGHT This detail shows an elaborate border, based upon a classic pattern popular in the Victorian era. Composed of pieces of veneer glued to solid tongue-and-groove planks, it is available by the foot.

BELOW LEFT For a more contemporary feeling, a border is fashioned by alternating light and dark segments of solid-wood planking.

BELOW RIGHT Ready-made borders are available for vinyl flooring that's made to look like wood.

OPPOSITE Borders can also be very simple. In this sunroom, two tones of wood plank are used to create a subtle border.

| | | | | | | | | | | | | | | floor your guests with borders | | | | | | | | | | | | | | |

Borders are another way to bring attention to your floors. They work in much the same way as a frame around a picture. Use them with just about any kind of flooring, including wood, stone, ceramic, vinyl, cork, and linoleum. Opt for ready-made patterns that range from floral to geometric designs, or compose your own. Border modules include straight sections and 90-degree turns for corners. Wood borders are available prefinished or unfinished, so you can match the stain and finish to your site-finished

borders

floor. When selecting borders, keep scale in mind. A wide, elaborate border may overpower a small room. If you are going to fill the room with furniture, you may be wise to skip the borders because you won't see much of them and they are costly—$10 to $70 per lineal foot (before installation), depending on design complexity. Save them for a large space or entry.

LEFT A basket-weave mosaic border, which matches the backsplash and field area above the range, is the perfect foil for the large field tiles in this kitchen.

OPPOSITE TOP LEFT Borders, also called listels, can be used to frame a room within a room, such as a conversation area.

OPPOSITE BOTTOM Even the simplest of borders—tiles in an analogous color and layed at a 45-degree angle to the other tiles in the room—give the room more interest.

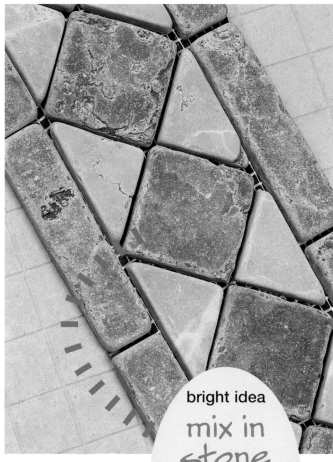

bright idea

mix in *stone*

Use a real stone border, such as this one, with a stone-like porcelain tile to enhance the overall effect.

Medallions make dramatic focal points, best suited to large floor areas where they can be seen. They are typically round or oval, but they're also available in octagonals, stars, and squares. They are created from exotic woods, marble, granite, limestone, onyx, and ceramics. Brass or aluminum inlay can be used to set off the shapes. Sizes usually range from 2 to 6 feet in diameter.

Wood medallions can be set into either solid or engineered wood floors. Computerized cutting machines make a wide variety of designs possible. Even small wood medallions can cost over $1,000. Check with the manufacturer about how the medallion finish will wear in traffic before you install one in your foyer.

Stone medallions are best suited to stone and ceramic floors. They typically come preassembled on mesh backings, allowing the joints to be grouted on site. Water jet technology, where water and an abrasive are shot through small nozzles at high pressure to create the desired cuts, have made such works of art more economically feasible—but they are still expensive. A 30-inch-diameter marble-and-granite medallion, for example, can easily cost $2,000. Labor to install it will add to the cost. Medallions can be created with other materials as well, including ceramic and glass tile or linoleum.

Decorative accents are a more subtle way to bring attention to your floors. They are smaller, often only a few inches square, and usually used in repetitive patterns. Otherwise, they are made using the same methods as medallions.

medallions and accents

ABOVE Most stone medallions are custom-made—not stock items—so homeowners can select materials that coordinate with their floor.

LEFT Variations on compass and rose motifs are popular for medallions in both stone and wood.

OPPOSITE TOP This wood medallion was site-finished to match the finish on the rest of the room's flooring.

BOTTOM LEFT Decorative wood accents are available in stock patterns, including this rose motif.

BOTTOM CENTER Decorative accents, such as this one, are fabricated using water-jet technology.

BOTTOM RIGHT Etched slate tiles are available in a variety of patterns and sizes. Custom designs are also an option.

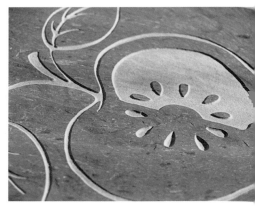

M osaic floors are composed of small pieces of colored stone, glass, tile, and other materials. They may be used to create interesting textures, patterns, or pictures. An ancient craft first popularized by the Greeks using pebbles and later by Romans using small tiles, mosaic floors often have a classical look.

mosaics

They can, however, be used in traditional, eclectic, and contemporary decorating schemes as well. Mosaics can be used to create borders, inlay strips (between larger field tiles), inserts (to replace larger tiles), and medallions. Pictorial subjects may include historical reproductions and a vast array of floral, animal, and celestial motifs. Mosaic tiles are sold individually or in preassembled motifs; set them with either mortar or adhesive. Some manufacturers allow you to design your own pattern, tile by tile. Then they ship it to you preassembled on a mesh backing or held together with a paper top sheet.

ABOVE RIGHT Versatile ceramic mosaics can be used to create free-form patterns, as in this contemporary bath.

RIGHT Patterns can be generated with computer design software and then preassembled in sections for easier installation.

OPPOSITE The mosaics in this shower have a baked-on finish that makes them resistant to lime deposits, dirt, and mold.

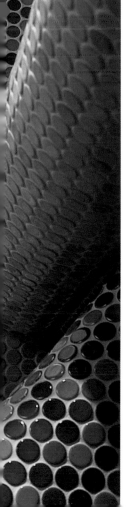

OPPOSITE Pictorial mosaics make interesting decorative accents in floors, especially when they are placed along a border.

LEFT Translucent glass mosaics sparkle against the opaque matte-finished field tiles in this foyer floor.

ABOVE Traditional white hexagonal mosaics, with borders and accents, evoke the turn of the last century in this kitchen.

BELOW Inexpensive accents in stone and ceramic transform a plain tile floor.

Many of the same effects described in previous sections can be simulated with latex paints, tints, and glazes. Called faux and trompe l'oeil painting (which translates from French as "false" and "trick of the eye," respectively), it takes some real skill to do effectively, but the results can be a lot of fun—and a lot less expensive than the real thing. Faux marble and faux wood inlay are done mostly on wood floors, but trompe l'oeil details, such as a sprig of flowers, can be painted on tile. Faux and trompe l'oeil painting, wherever it's done, should be protected with several coats of polyurethane.

painted floors and floor cloths

For the Colonial look, painted floor cloths are appropriate over any hard-surface flooring. (Placed over carpet, the paint may crack.) Painted on latex-primed canvas or on carpeting, this is a project that even a first-time do-it-yourselfer can do. Not an artist? Mylar stencils are available in patterns reproduced from historic New England homes. Hand-painted floor cloths can also be purchased in both historical and contemporary designs. Painted floor cloths are durable but should regularly be protected with a thin coat of paste wax.

bright idea
draw an ace

Use spray paint or a brush to create a unique sisal rug. For more "carpet art" ideas, see page 180.

TOP AND ABOVE Draw from your child's favorite things when seeking inspiration for a motif in a child's room.

RIGHT It doesn't take many painted accents to transform a floor, as this star- and diamond-studded entryway proves.

OPPOSITE This trompe l'oeil "rug" features a magazine cover resting on it.

RIGHT Two shades of stain over a natural field were used to create this charming bedroom floor.

BELOW A diamond pattern, in contrasting stains, separates the foyer from the dining room beyond.

BELOW RIGHT This crossing pattern is achieved with paint thinned to transparency.

customize a carpet

1 **To make a stencil,** draw your pattern on cardboard. Use grid lines to help keep the pattern even and consistent. Then cut out the stencil using a utility knife, and attach double-sided tape to the back.

2 **Attach the stencil** to the carpet or floor cloth, and shield adjacent areas. Tape over stencil openings that will be painted with a different color. Spray lightly and briefly, only enough to cover.

3 **If using more than one color,** repeat the previous two steps. To create straight, uniform borders, use tape to mark crisp edges and to protect the rest of the carpet. Spray lightly but consistently to achieve the same color throughout.

4 **When the last coat is dry,** lift off the tape, paper, and stencil carefully to reveal the finished design. As with this example, paint often looks most striking on light-colored carpet.

LEFT This floral embellishment was made with a purchased stencil, best for more intricate designs and for those of us with less time or patience.

RIGHT This attractive floor covering began as an inexpensive piece of wall-to-wall carpeting. The same techniques apply to creating a floor cloth.

BELOW A rug or floor cloth that can incorporate the existing colors, themes, and scale of a room may be easier and more affordable to make than find.

BELOW RIGHT Inspiration for painted floor coverings can come from fine art hanging in museums or from a painting or print that is hanging over your fireplace.

IIIIIIIIIIIIIIIIIIIIIIIIIIII transform a plain carpet IIIIIIIIIIIIIIIIIIIIIIIII

LEFT Floor cloths were popular during Colonial times, when many homeowners were unable to afford woven rugs. They continue to be a natural fit for period decor, such as in this dining room.

BELOW LEFT Floor cloths were also used in wealthy homes to protect more-expensive floors. This galley kitchen runner serves the same purpose today.

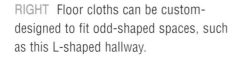

RIGHT Floor cloths can be custom-designed to fit odd-shaped spaces, such as this L-shaped hallway.

ABOVE LEFT Inspiration for floor cloths can come from anywhere. This one was based on a grill carved from marble that the artist saw at a museum in Greece. The hems were glued, and several coats of polyurethane were applied for protection.

ABOVE RIGHT The first step in creating this floor cloth was to prime heavy-duty canvas with interior latex primer. The faux marble and the motif were then painted by hand using artist-grade acrylic paints.

BELOW This large, seashore-themed floor cloth was hung on a wall to make it easier to paint. Smaller cloths can be stretched on stretcher sticks (used for artist's canvases) for painting.

Resource Guide

MANUFACTURERS

828 International Trading Co.
1512-A Roper Mountain Rd.
Greenville, SC 29615
800-733-0828
www.828rugs.com
Manufactures hand-tufted and power-loomed rugs.

Alloc
3441 South Memorial Dr.
Racine, WI 53403
877-362-5562
www.alloc.com
Manufactures engineered hardwood flooring.

Ambient Bamboo Products, Inc.
866-710-7070
www.ambientbp.com
Manufactures bamboo flooring.

American Olean Tile Co.
1000 Cannon Ave.
Lansdale, PA 19446-0271
215-855-1111
www.americanolean.com
Manufactures ceramic tile.

Amtico International Inc.
6480 Roswell Road
Atlanta, GA 30328
404-267-1900
www.amtico.com
Manufactures vinyl flooring.

Ancestral Floors
875 98th St.
St. Georges, Quebec, Canada G5Y 8G2
418-227-3788
800-493-3788
www.ancestralfloors.com
Manufactures preoiled wood flooring.

Armstrong World Industries, Inc.
Attn: Consumer Solution Center
P.O. Box 3001
Lancaster, PA 17604
800-233-3823
www.armstrong.com
Manufactures vinyl, high-pressure plastic laminate, and linoleum.

Award Hardwood Floors, LLP
401 North 72nd Ave.
Wausau, WI 54401
715-849-8080
888-862-9273
www.awardfloors.com
Manufactures hardwood floors.

The following list of manufacturers and associations is meant to be a general guide to additional industry and product-related sources. It is not intended as a listing of products and manufacturers represented by the photographs in this book.

Bruce Hardwood Floors (div. of Armstrong)
16803 Dallas Parkway
Addison, TX 75001
800-722-4647
www.bruce.com
Manufactures solid wood, engineered hardwood, and high-pressure plastic laminate.

Congoleum Corp.
Dept. C
P.O. Box 3127
Mercerville, NJ 08619-0127
800-274-3266
www.congoleum.com
Munufactures resilient, high-pressure plastic laminate flooring.

Resource Guide

Couristan, Inc.
2 Executive Dr.
Fort Lee, NJ 07024
800-223-6186
www.couristan.com
Manufactures natural and synthetic carpets and rugs.

Deutsche Steinzeug America, Inc.
Jasba Tile
367 Curie Dr.
Alpharetta, GA 30005
770-442-5500
www.dsa-ceramics.com
www.jasba.de
Manufactures ceramic tile.

DRIcore Subfloor System
2311 Royal Windsor Dr., Unit 2
Mississauga, Ontario, Canada L5J 1K5
888-566-4522
www.dricore.com
Manufactures subfloor systems.

EGS Electrical Group
Easy Heat
2 Connecticut South Dr.
East Granby, CT 06026
860-653-1600
www.easyheat.com
Manufactures floor warming systems.

Edge Flooring, LLC
200 Howell Dr.
Dalton, GA 30721
706-226-3343
www.edgeflooring.com
Manufactures laminate tile flooring.

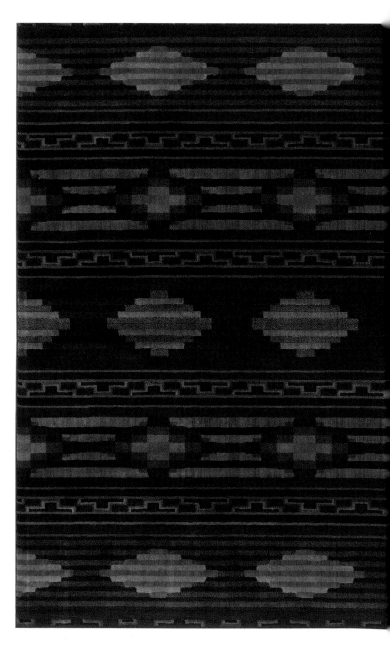

Elmwood Reclaimed Timber

P.O. Box 10750

Kansas City, MO 64188-0750

816-532-0300

800-705-0705

www.elmwoodreclaimedtimber.com

Provides reclaimed timber and stone products.

Expanko, Inc.

3135 Lower Valley Rd.

Parkesburg, PA 19365

800-345-6202

www.expanko.com

Manufactures cork and rubber flooring.

F. Schumacher & Co.

1325 Old Cooches Bridge Rd.

P.O. Box 6002

Newark, DE 19714

302-454-3200

www.fschumacher.com

Manufactures carpets and area rugs.

Filmtech, LLC

877-345-6832

www.filmtechonline.com

Manufactures surface protection products.

Flexco Floors

1401 East 6th St.

Tuscumbia, AL 35674

800-633-3151

www.flexcofloors.com

Manufactures rubber and vinyl flooring.

Forbo Linoleum Inc.

Humboldt Industrial Park

P.O. Box 667

Hazleton, PA 18201

570-459-0771

www.forbolinoleumna.com

Manufactures linoleum flooring.

Gladiator GarageWorks

2000 M-63 North

Benton Harbor, MI 49022

866-342-4089

www.gladiatorgw.com

Manufactures garage flooring and storage accessories.

Globus Cork

741 East 136th St.

Bronx, NY 10454

718-742-7264

www.corkfloor.com

Manufactures cork flooring.

Resource Guide

Gobbetto S.R.L.
Via Carroccio 16
20123 Milan - Italy
U.S. contact - 203-918-4971
www.gobbetto.com
Manufactures and installs resin floors and coatings.

Godfrey Hirst Carpets
#118B/1000 Holcomb Woods Parkway
Roswell, GA 30076
678-461-7545
www.godfreyhirst.com
Manufactures wool and synthetic carpets and area rugs.

Gracewood Design
707 18th St.
San Francisco, CA 94107
415-695-1480
www.gracewooddesign.com
Custom designs painted floor cloths, hardwood and concrete floors.

Green Mountain Soapstone Corp.
680 East Hubbardton Rd.
P.O. Box 807
Castleton, VT 05735
802-468-5636
www.greenmountainsoapstone.com
Manufactures soapstone floors, walls, sinks, and countertops.

Hagaman Carpet Industries
208 Second St.
Ft. Oglethorpe, GA 30742
706-861-6028
800-448-0279
www.hagamancarpet.com
Manufactures synthetic and natural carpets.

Hartco Hardwood Floors (div. of Armstrong)
P.O. Box 4009
Oneida, TN 37841
800-769-8528
www.hartcoflooring.com
Manufactures engineered hardwood and solid wood flooring.

Helios, a div. of Mohawk Industries
500 Town Park Lane, Suite 400
Kennesaw, GA 30144
800-843-5138
www.helioscarpet.com
Manufactures wool carpets and area rugs.

InterfaceFLOR
116 North York Rd., Suite 300
Elmhurst, IL 60126
866-281-3567
www.interfaceflor.com
Manufactures nylon and natural fiber carpet tiles.

International Vinyl Co.

200 Munekata Dr.

Dalton, GA 30721

706-278-8008

www.ivcgroup.com

Manufactures fiberglass-reinforced vinyl flooring.

Island Stone North America

P.O. Box 400

Capitola, CA 95010

800-371-0001

www.islandstonena.com

Manufactures natural stone and glass tiles.

James Hardie Building Products

26300 La Alameda, Suite 250

Mission Viejo, CA 92691

888-J-HARDIE

www.jameshardie.com

Manufactures cement backer board and other building products.

Jason Robert's Inc.

Milford, CT 06460

800-801-7587

www.jasonrobertsinc.net

Creates decorative concrete and polymer-reinforced cement floors.

Jian & Ling Bamboo

#107 – 2601 Reliance Dr.

Virginia Beach, VA 23452

757-368-2060

www.jianlingbamboo.com

Manufactures vertical and horizontal cut bamboo flooring.

Kährs International Inc.

940 Centre Circle #1000

Altamonte Springs, FL 32714

800-800-KAHR

www.kahrs.com

Manufactures engineered hardwood flooring.

Resource Guide

Karen Kernan

576 Leetes Island Rd.

Stony Creek, CT 06405

203-481-0254

www.karenkernan.com

Designs floor cloths.

Kemiko Concrete Products

P.O. Box 1109

Leonard, TX 75452-3677

903-587-3708

www.kemiko.com

Manufactures acid stains for concrete flooring and other concrete products. Creates decorative concrete floors.

Klutch Design, LLC

262 Quarry Rd.

Milford, CT 06460

203-878-6411

www.klutchdesign.com

Designs and manufactures stone medallions, borders, and accents.

Laticrete International, Inc.

1 Laticrete Park North

Bethany, CT 06524-3423

203-393-0010

800-243-4788

www.laticrete.com

Manufactures epoxy grout in many colors.

Mannington Mills, Inc.

75 Mannington Mills Rd.

Salem, NJ 08079

856-935-3000

www.mannington.com

Manufactures resilient, engineered hardwood, porcelain, and high-pressure plastic laminate flooring.

Mirage

1255-98th St.

St. Georges, Quebec, Canada G5Y 8J5

418-227-1181

www.miragefloors.com

Manufactures prefinished engineered hardwood flooring.

Mohawk Industries, Inc.

160 South Industrial Blvd.

Calhoun, GA 30701

1-800-266-4295

www.mohawkflooring.com

Manufactures broadloom carpeting, area rugs, hardwood, laminate, ceramic tile and vinyl flooring.

Momeni

36 East 31st St.

New York, NY 10016

212-532-9577

www.momeni.com

Manufactures natural and synthetic carpets and area rugs.

Nuheat Industries, Ltd.

1689 Cliveden Ave.

Delta, British Columbia, Canada V3M 6V5

800-778-WARM

www.nuheat.com

Manufactures radiant electric floor heating systems.

Pergo, Inc.

Attention: Consumer Affairs

3128 Highwoods Blvd., Suite 100

Raleigh, NC 27604

800-337-3746

www.pergo.com

Manufactures high-pressure plastic laminate flooring.

Proflex Products Inc.

3406 Dean St.

Naples, FL 34104

877-538-3437

www.proflexcism.com

Manufactures sound control, crack isolation, and waterproofing membranes.

Quick-Step, Inc.

550 Cloniger Dr.

Thomasville, NC 27360

866-220-5933

www.quick-step.com

Manufactures glue-less laminate flooring.

Robbins Hardwood (div. of Armstrong)

16803 Dallas Parkway

Addison, TX 75001

800-733-3309

www.robbins.com

Manufactures solid wood flooring.

Resource Guide

Rodeo Carpet Mills
5900 East Slauson Ave.
Commerce, CA 90040
800-533-3292
www.rodeocarpet.com
Manufactures carpets and area rugs.

Royal Dutch Carpet, a div. of Stanton Carpet Corp.
300 Union Grove Rd.
Calhoun, GA 30701
800-452-4474
www.stantoncarpet.com
Manufactures carpets and area rugs.

Shaw Industries, Inc.
616 East Walnut Ave.
Dalton, GA 30722-2128
800-441-7429
www.shawinc.com
Manufactures carpet, hardwood, laminate, and porcelain flooring.

Silver Creek (div. of Bloomsburg Carpet Industries)
49 West 23rd St., 4th Floor
New York, NY 10010
212-688-7447
www.bloomsburgcarpet.com
Manufactures wool carpeting.

Stark Carpet Corp.
979 Third Ave.
New York, NY 10022
212-752-9000
www.starkcarpet.com
Manufactures carpet, textiles, wall coverings, and fine furniture (available through interior designers only).

Tarkett
www.tarkett-floors.com
Addresses and phone numbers for each product division are listed on the Web site.
Manufactures vinyl, laminate, tile, and wood flooring.

Teragren
12715 Miller Rd. NE, Suite 301
Bainbridge Island, WA 98110
800-929-6333
206-842-9477
www.teragren.com
Manufactures bamboo flooring, panels, and veneers.

Unique Carpets, Ltd.
7360 Jurupa Ave.
Riverside, CA 92504
951-352-8125
www.uniquecarpetsltd.com
Manufactures wool, sisal, and synthetic carpets.

Van Dijk Carpet, Inc.

P.O. Box 1569

Cartersville, GA 30120

770-382-4984, 800-222-9005

or 800-476-8323

www.vandijkcarpet.com

Manufactures natural and synthetic carpets and floor coverings.

Vifah Vietnamese Fine Furniture

Snapping Tile ™

P.O. Box 2057

New York, NY 10159

718-383-5406

www.vifah.com

Manufactures wood tiles attached to a polypropylene base that snap together.

Warmly Yours

2 Corporate Dr., Suite 100

Lake Zurich, IL 60047

800-875-5285

www.warmlyyours.com

Manufactures radiant floor heating systems.

Wilsonart International Inc.

2400 Wilson Pl.

Temple, TX 76503

800-433-3222

www.wilsonart.com

Manufactures high-pressure plastic laminate flooring.

Wools of New Zealand

P.O. Box 172

Marble Hill, GA 30148

800-367-0462

www.woolcarpet.com

Manufactures wool broadloom carpets and area rugs.

Resource Guide

FLOOR CARE PRODUCTS

BonaKemi USA, Inc.
14805 Moncrieff Pl.
Aurora, CO 80011
www.bonakemi.com

INSTITUTES AND ASSOCIATIONS

American Academy of Family Physicians
P.O. Box 11210
Shawnee Mission, KS 66207-1210
800-274-2237
www.aafp.org
Recommendations for allergy sufferers.

Carpet and Rug Institute (CRI)
P.O. Box 2048
Dalton, GA 30722-2048
706-278-3176
www.carpet-rug.com
Carpet and rug information resources.

Hardwood Information Center
400 Penn Center Blvd., Suite 530
Pittsburgh, PA 15235
800-373-WOOD
www.hardwood.org
Hardwood flooring information and resources.

Masonry Institute of America

22815 Frampton Ave.

Torrance, CA 90501-5034

800-221-4000

www.masonryinstitute.org

Masonry information and resources.

National Safety Council

1121 Spring Lake Dr.

Itasca, IL 60143-3201

800-621-7619

630-285-1121

www.nsc.org

Recommendations to avoid slips and falls.

National Terrazzo and Mosaic Association

201 North Maple Ave., Suite 208

Purcellville, VA 20132

540-751-0930

800-323-9736

www.ntma.com

Terrazzo and mosaic information and resources.

NOFMA: The Wood Flooring Manufacturers Association

P.O. Box 3009

Memphis, TN 38173-0009

www.nofma.com

901-526-5016

Information about wood floors and floor grading.

Resilient Floor Covering Institute

401 East Jefferson Street, Suite 102

Rockville, MD 20850

301-340-8580

www.rfci.com

Resilient flooring information and resources.

Tile Council of North America, Inc. (TCNA)

100 Clemson Research Center

Anderson, SC 29625

864-646-8453

www.tileusa.com

Tile information and resources.

World Floor Covering Association

2211 East Howell Ave.

Anaheim, CA 92806

800-624-6880

www.wfca.org

In-depth information on all types of flooring.

Glossary

Acclimatization: Storing flooring on site to adjust to local humidity levels, which helps prevent future shrinking, swelling, or buckling; especially important with wood floors.

Asbestos: Mineral fiber harmful to the lungs commonly used in older construction materials, including floor tiles and flooring adhesive; removing or abrading these materials can release fibers into the air and should be avoided.

Baseboard molding: Decorative

molding made of wood, resin, or MDF (medium density fiberboard); finishes and protects walls where they meet the floor and conceals floor expansion joints.

Border: A stripe or more elaborate design that runs around the perimeter of a floor; serves as a frame or accent. Available ready-made in many materials, including wood, ceramic, vinyl, and linoleum.

Caulk: A material used to seal joints between tile flooring and walls, bathtubs, cabinets, etc., or as a filler to be painted; usually silicone-, latex-, or acrylic-based.

Cement backer board: Cement and fiberglass mesh sheets used to cover wood subfloors before laying ceramic or stone tile.

Ceramic tile: Tiles made of natural clay and baked in a kiln; more porous than porcelain tiles.

Engineered wood: Flooring made up of thin plies of wood and topped with a hardwood veneer.

Epoxy: Bonding substance made of thermosetting resins that is water- and chemical-resistant, and durable; typically used as a skid-resistant floor coating over concrete or as an adhesive and grout for tiles.

Faux: Simulates expensive flooring, such as marble, with paints, tints, and glazes.

Feather: To create a smooth transition from one surface level to another by

means of a filler, such as patching compound; useful when preparing for installation of a new floor over an old floor or slab.

Fiberboard: Wood or vegetable fibers bonded together and compressed into sheets or used as the core for various types of flooring; comes in various densities.

Fiberglass: Material made from extremely fine fibers of glass; some reinforced vinyl flooring contains fiberglass to minimize expansion and contraction.

Grout: A material used to fill in the spaces between tiles; most commonly made from Portland cement but also can be silicone-based; available in different colors.

Laminate flooring: A tongue-and-groove interlocking system of flooring that floats above the subfloor; consists of a decorative resin surface coated with aluminum oxide over a wood composite core.

Medallion: A decorative inlay pattern, usually set in an oval or circular frame.

Mohs scale: A rating of a surface's ability to withstand scratches on a scale of 1-10, 10 being the hardness of a diamond; named after Frederick Mohs, a German mineralogist.

Moisture test: Using a meter to determine moisture content of a slab, subfloor, or flooring material; helps to ensure a successful installation by preventing future swelling, shrinking, and buckling.

Mortar: A compound of cement, sand, water, and possibly lime, usually used to provide a stable, level base for stone or ceramic tile.

Mosaic tiles: Tiles 2 inches square or less, glazed or unglazed, that are installed individually or prearranged on mesh sheets; can be used to make intricate designs or images.

Outgassing: Releasing vapors at room temperature; VOCs (volatile organic compounds) outgas very readily and can be harmful to people and the environment.

Overlayment: Typically refers to the application of a polymer reinforced cement layer to level, repair, or decorate an existing floor.

Padding: Carpet underlay made of rebond (high density foam), slab rubber, fiber (jute or synthetic), or frothed foam (high-density polyurethane) that makes carpeting more comfortable, durable, and resilient.

Parquet: Flooring composed of small wood slats joined by adhesive and fasteners; typically square.

P.E.I. scale: The Porcelain Enamel Institute rating system that measures a tile's resistance to abrasion on a scale of I to V, V being hard enough for commercial, high-traffic situations.

Polyurethane: Developed as a synthetic substitute for rubber; as a foam it provides cushioning, durability, noise reduction, and insulation under carpeting. May also be applied as a coating to protect some floors, such as wood, cork, and bamboo.

Porcelain flooring: Tiles made by firing fine-particulate clay and minerals at high temperatures; harder, denser, and less absorbant than ceramic tiles.

Portland cement: A material made of lime and clay combined with sand; hardens and becomes water-resistant when mixed with water.

Resilient flooring: Flooring that has a  firm surface but that will also "give" slightly and "bounce back" to its original shape after being compressed, such as by a piece of furniture. Includes vinyl, linoleum, rubber, and cork and is known for durability, comfort, moisture resistance, noise reduction, and ease of cleaning.

Sealant: A product applied over more porous flooring (tile, concrete, stone, etc.) to protect it from moisture and staining, and to make cleaning easier.

Shim: A thin, tapered strip of wood, or pieces of building paper, used to raise the height of subflooring to level.

Stencil: A sheet of heavy paper or Mylar with a cutout design; paint is applied through the cutouts with a stencil brush to create patterns.

Terra cotta: Porous tiles made from raw clay that range in color from warm red-browns to roses and oranges; may need to be sealed to lessen water absorption.

Terrazzo: Composite material made of marble, quartz, granite, or glass chips (usually quarry waste material) and bound with cements or epoxies that can be poured like concrete or made into tiles.

Threshold: A wood, metal, or stone

material nailed or screwed to the floor, typically at entryways; often acts as a transition between flooring of different materials and/or heights.

Tongue-and-groove: Reciprocal profiles

milled on wood or laminate strips and planks that fit together and produce strong joints.

Transition: Wood, metal, or stone nailed

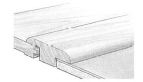

or screwed to the floor between two types of flooring materials.

Trompe l'oeil: Painted details or vistas done with the intention of momentarily fooling the viewer; typically done on walls but sometimes seen on flooring, such as a medallion that's painted to look as if it were inlaid.

Underlayment: Material installed over a subfloor and under a finished floor; may be used to prevent transmission of moisture or sound, to smooth a rough subsurface, or to provide a degree of cushioning.

Vapor barrier: A material (paper, plastic, metal, or paint) used to prevent the passage of moisture, such as from a concrete slab to the flooring above.

Veneer: A decorative top layer of attractively grained wood that is glued to layers of inferior materials.

VOCs (volatile organic compounds): Chemicals containing carbon at a molecular level that easily form vapors at room temperature; some flooring and flooring adhesives emit VOCs, which can be potentially harmful to people and the environment.

Water jet: A method of cutting stone or tile using water and abrasive shot through small nozzles at high pressure; used to cut intricate patterns.

Wet Saw: A saw, available at rental outlets, used to cut ceramic and stone tiles.

Index

Index

Index

Photo Credits

T: Top R: Right B: Bottom L: Left C: Center

page 1: courtesy of Bruce Hardwood/Armstrong page 3: courtesy of Island Stone page 4: courtesy of Mannington page 6: (*TL*) courtesy of Armstrong (*R*) courtesy of Forbo (*BL*) courtesy of Teragren page 8: Robert Perron pages 10-11: (*TL*) courtesy of Hartco/Armstrong (*BL*) courtesy of Bruce Laminate/Armstrong (*TR*) Robert Perron (*BR*) courtesy of Shaw pages 12-13: (*TL*) courtesy of Mannington (*BL*) Carl Weese (*TR*) courtesy of IVC (*BR*) courtesy of Stanton pages 14-15: (*C*) Carl Weese (*TR*) Robert Perron (*BR*) Mark Samu pages 16-17: (*TL*) courtesy of Hartco/Armstrong (*BL, BC*) Robert Perron (*BR*) courtesy of Quick-Step pages 18-19: (*TL*) courtesy of Mannington (*BL*) courtesy of Armstrong (*C, BR*) Robert Perron (*TR*) Mark Samu pages 20-21: (*TL, CL, TR*) courtesy of Armstrong (*BL*) courtesy of Couristan (*BR*) courtesy of Shaw pages 22: Home and Garden Editorial Services pages 24-25: (*BC*) courtesy of Shaw (*TC*) courtesy of Quick-Step pages 26-27: (*TL*) Home and Garden Editorial Services (*BL*) Robert Perron (*C*) courtesy of Forbo (*R*) courtesy of Kemiko pages 28-29: (*TL, BR*) courtesy of Armstrong (*BL*) courtesy of Stanton (*TC*) Robert Perron (*TR*) courtesy of Teragren pages 30-31: (*TL*) courtesy of Mohawk (*TC, BL*) courtesy of Flexco (*BR*) courtesy of Hartco/Armstrong pages 32-33: (*TL*) courtesy of Mohawk (*BL*) courtesy of Green Mountain Soapstone (*TC*) Robert Perron (*BC*) Home and Garden Editorial Services pages 34-35: (*TL, R*) courtesy of Mannington (*BC*) Home and Garden Editorial Services pages 36-37: courtesy of Robbins/Armstrong pages 38-39: (*TC, BC*) Robert Perron (*BR*) courtesy of Hartco/Armstrong pages 40-41: (*C*) courtesy of Hartco/Armstrong (*TR,BR*) Home

and Garden Editorial Services pages 42-43: (*C*) Robert Perron (*TL, BR*) courtesy of Shaw (*BC*) courtesy of Hartco/Armstrong pages 44-45: (*TL*) courtesy of Elmwood Reclaimed Timber (*TC*) courtesy of Hartco/Armstrong (*TR*) courtesy of Robbins/Armstrong (*BR*) courtesy of Shaw pages 46-47: (*L, C, BR*) courtesy of Teragren (*TR*) Home and Garden Editorial Services pages 48-49: courtesy of Teragren pages 50-51: courtesy of Expanko pages 52-53: courtesy of Expanko pages 54-55: (*TC, BC, TR*) courtesy of Forbo (*BR*) courtesy of Armstrong pages 56-57: courtesy of Forbo page 58: (*T 2 photos*) courtesy of Karastan (*B 2 photos*) courtesy of Momeni page 59: Robert Perron page 60: Robert Perron page 61: (*T*) courtesy of F. Schumacher (*CT*) courtesy of Glen Eden (*CB*) courtesy of Silver Creek (*B*) courtesy of Rodeo Carpet Mills pages 62-63: (*TL, BC*) courtesy of Robbins/Armstrong (*BL, TR, BR*) courtesy of Stark pages 64-65: (*TL, BL*) Robert Perron (*TC, TR, BR*) Home and Garden Editorial Services pages 66-67: courtesy of Mannington pages 68-69: (*L*) Home and Garden Editorial Services (*C*) courtesy of Green Mountain Soapstone (*R*) Robert Perron pages 70-71: (*TL, TR*) Robert Perron (*BL*) Mark Samu (*BR*) Home and Garden Editorial Services pages 72-73: (*L*) courtesy of Island Stone (*R*) Home and Garden Editorial Services pages 74-75: (*L, CR, BR*) courtesy of Kemiko (*TC, BC*) courtesy of Jason Robert's Inc. pages 76-77: (*L, TC, BC*) courtesy of Kemiko (*BR 2 photos*) courtesy of Gobbetto pages 78-79: (*C, BR*) courtesy of Armstrong (*BL 2 photos, TR*) courtesy of Mannington pages 80-81: (*TL*) courtesy of Mannington (*BL 6 photos, TR*) Home and Garden Editorial Services (*BR*) Mark Samu pages 82-83: (*C*) Home and Garden Editorial Services (*R 4 photos*) courtesy of Edge Flooring pages 84-85: courtesy

of Mannington pages 86-87: (*TL, BL, TR*) courtesy of Mannington (*BC, BR*) courtesy of Armstrong pages 88-89: (*TL, BC*) courtesy of Armstrong (*BL*) courtesy of Mannington (*CR*) courtesy of Quick-Step (*BR*) Home and Garden Editorial Services pages 90-91: courtesy of Armstrong pages 92-93: (*TL*) courtesy of IVC (*C*) courtesy of Armstrong (*BR*) Home and Garden Editorial Services pages 94-95: courtesy of Armstrong pages 96-97: (*TL*) courtesy of Armstrong (*BL, BC, BR*) courtesy of Mannington (*TR 3 photos*) Home and Garden Editorial Services pages 98-99: (*TL, BL*) courtesy of Gladiator (*BC, BR*) courtesy of Flexco (*TR 2 photos*) Home and Garden Editorial Services pages 100-101: (*L*) courtesy of Shaw (*TR*) courtesy of Unique Carpets, Ltd. (*BR*) courtesy of Helios pages 102-103: (*L*) courtesy of Mohawk (*R 4 photos*) Home and Garden Editorial Services pages 104-105: (*L 4 photos, TR*) Home and Garden Editorial Services (*BC*) courtesy of Mohawk (*BR*) courtesy of InterfaceFLOR pages 106-107: courtesy of Mannington pages 108-109: (*TL*) courtesy of Expanko (*BL*) courtesy of Quickstep (*BR*) Mark Samu pages 110-111: (*TL, BR*) courtesy of Armstrong (*BL*) courtesy of Forbo (*BC, TR*) Robert Perron pages 112-113: (*TL*) courtesy of Mannington (*BL*) Mark Samu (*R*) courtesy of Green Mountain Soapstone pages 114-115: (*TL*) Mark Samu (*BL*) George Ross/CH (*TR, BR*) courtesy of Armstrong pages 116-117: (*TL, C*) courtesy of Jasba Tile (*BL*) courtesy of Island Stone (*R 3 photos*) courtesy of Nuheat pages 118-119: (*L*) courtesy of Mannington (*BC*) courtesy of Whirlpool (*TR, BR*) Mark Samu pages 120-121: courtesy of Shaw pages 122-123: (*L*) courtesy of Mannington (*TR, BR*) courtesy of Hartco/Armstrong (*BC*) courtesy of Bruce/Armstrong pages 124-125: (*TL*) courtesy of Mohawk (*TC, TR*) courtesy of Mannington (*BC*) courtesy of Shaw (*BR*) courtesy of Forbo **pages 126-127:** (*TC*) Robert Perron (*BL*) courtesy of Robbins/Armstrong (*BC*) Home and Garden Editorial Services (*R*) courtesy of Tarkett **pages 128-129:** (*TL*) courtesy of Hartco/Armstrong (*BL, BR*) courtesy of Armstrong (*BC*) Robert Perron **pages 130-131:** (*L*) courtesy of Mannington (*TR*) courtesy of Tarkett (*BR*) courtesy of Shaw **pages 132-133:** (*BL*) courtesy of Godfrey Hirst (*T, BR*) courtesy of Armstrong (*CR*) Home and Garden Editorial Services (*CL*) courtesy of Robbins/Armstrong **pages 134-135:** (*TL, BL*) courtesy of Armstrong (*BC*) courtesy of Mannington (*TR*) courtesy of Filmtech (*BR*) courtesy of Shaw **pages 136-137:** (*BL, BR*) courtesy of IVC (*BC*) courtesy of Mohawk (*TR*) courtesy of Armstrong **pages 138-139:** (*L,TR*) courtesy of Mannington (*BR*) courtesy of Kemiko **pages 140-141:** (*BL*) courtesy of Ambient (*C*) courtesy of Mannington (*R*) Robert Perron **pages 142-143:** (*TL, R*) Robert Perron (*BL*) courtesy of Mannington **pages 144-145:** Robert Perron **pages 146-147:** (*TL, R*) Robert Perron (*BL*) courtesy of Mannington **pages 148-149:** (*L, BR*) courtesy of Mannington (*TC, BC, TR*) Robert Perron **pages 150-151:** (*L*) courtesy of Forbo (*TR*) courtesy of Teragren (*BR*) Robert Perron **pages 152-153:** (*L, BR*) courtesy of Shaw (*TC*) Mark Samu (*TR*) Home and Garden Editorial Services **pages 154-155:** (*T*) courtesy of Kemiko (*BL*) courtesy of Gladiator (*BR*) courtesy of Jason Robert's Inc. **pages 156-157:** (*L 3 photos, T*) courtesy of DRIcore (*B*) courtesy of Mannington **pages 158-159:** Robert Perron **pages 160-161:** (*L*) courtesy of Shaw (*TR*) courtesy of Expanko (*BR*) courtesy of Armstrong **pages 162-163:** (*TL*) courtesy of Crossville (*BL, R*) courtesy of Mannington (*BC 2 photos*) courtesy of

Armstrong **pages 164-165:** (*L 4 photos, BC*) Lars Dalsgaard (*TC*) Peter Bleyer (*R*) courtesy of Forbo **pages 166-167:** (*BL*) courtesy of Mannington (*TC, BC*) Home and Garden Editorial Services (*BR*) courtesy of Hartco/Armstrong **pages 168-169:** (*L*) courtesy of Crossville (*TC*) courtesy of Armstrong (*TR*) Home and Garden Editorial Services (*BR*) courtesy of Mannington **pages 170-171:** (*BL, C, BR 3 photos*) Home and Garden Editorial Services (*TR*) Robert Perron **pages 172-173:** courtesy of Jasba **pages 174-175:** (*L*) Home and Garden Editorial Services (*C, TR*) Mark Samu (*BR*)

Carl Weese **pages 176-177:** (*C, TR 2 photos*) Mark Samu (*BR*) Carl Weese **pages 178-179:** (*L*) Robert Perron (*TR, BC, BR*) Mark Samu **pages 180-181:** Lars Dalsgaard **page 182:** courtesy of Gracewood Designs **page 183:** Sean Kernan **page 185:** courtesy of Teragren **page 186:** courtesy of Shaw **page 189:** courtesy of Expanko **page 190:** courtesy of Hartco/Armstrong **page 193:** courtesy of Forbo **page 194:** courtesy of Shaw **page 195:** Robert Perron **page 196:** courtesy of Hartco/Armstrong **page 197:** courtesy of Award **page 207:** courtesy of Armstrong

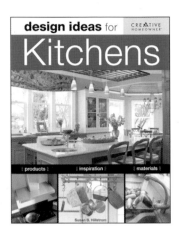
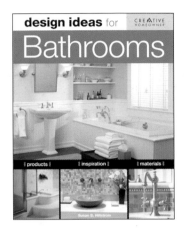
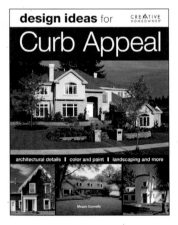
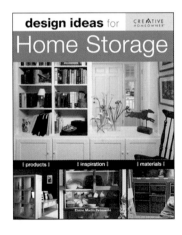